# More Social Studies Through Children's Literature

## An Integrated Approach

Anthony D. Fredericks

Associate Professor of Education
York College
York, Pennsylvania

Illustrated by Rebecca N. Fredericks

2000
Teacher Ideas Press
A Division of
Libraries Unlimited, Inc.
Englewood, Colorado

TEACHER IDEAS PRESS
A Division of
Libraries Unlimited, Inc.
P.O. Box 6633
Englewood, CO 80155-6633
1-800-237-6124
www.lu.com/tip

**Library of Congress Cataloging-in-Publication Data**

Fredericks, Anthony D.
    More social studies through children's literature : an integrated approach / Anthony D. Fredericks
       p. cm.
    Includes bibliographical references and index.
    ISBN 1-56308-761-8
    1. Social sciences--Study and teaching (Elementary)--United States.  2. Children's
literature--Study and teaching (Elementary)--United States.  3. Language experience
approach in education--United States.  I. Title.
LB1584.F659 1999
372.83044--dc21

                                  99-041002
                                     CIP

# *Dedication*

*To Brian Glandon*
*for his endearing camaraderie,*
*continuous support,*
*and ever-present humor!*

# Contents

# *Figures and Tables*

## Figures

## Tables

# *Preface*

Who would have thought? When I wrote *Social Studies Through Children's Literature* in 1991, I was not prepared for the overwhelming and enthusiastic response it got from thousands of teachers all across the country. Teachers from urban, suburban, and rural schools eagerly purchased copies of that book and joyfully shared the activities and projects with their students, revitalizing their social studies curricula in a plethora of creative and dynamic ways. Conversations with educators in school districts all over the United States confirmed that a rich vein had been tapped—a vein of curricular gold that reinvigorated both the teaching and learning of social studies.

To say that I was delighted and thrilled would be an understatement. Scores of letters and e-mail messages from new and experienced teachers alike supported a literature-based social studies curriculum as just the ticket for moving students beyond textbook learning and into a hands-on, minds-on approach to education that connects them with the world in which they live. Making homemade oatmeal muffins (*Sam Johnson and the Blue Ribbon Quilt*) supplanted mindless workbook sheets; building a classroom terrarium (*The Great Kapok Tree*) took the place of vapid question-and-answer sessions; and inviting students to create period costumes (*Miss Rumphius*) replaced round robin reading from out-of-date textbooks. Teachers were excited about teaching social studies; students were excited about learning social studies. Who would have thought?

Since that book was first published, social studies education has changed remarkably. New standards issued by the National Council on the Social Studies, fresh new trade books written by some of this country's most exciting authors, mind-boggling new Web sites, and a reconfiguration of social studies curricula all across the country are indicative of the exciting changes and transformations taking place. I wanted to share that enthusiasm and energy once again in a follow-up book that would share *new* literature and *new* ideas with classroom teachers—a book that would build upon and extend the successes, excitement, and exhilaration enjoyed by teachers who energetically embraced *Social Studies Through Children's Literature*.

This book, like the first, is designed to offer you a participatory approach to social studies education—an approach saying that when students enjoy meaningful opportunities to make an *investment of self* in their education, that education will become both relevant and dynamic. Thus, the emphasis in this book (as it was in the first) is on the *processes* of learning, not the *products*. This book does not replace the first, but complements it. It offers new literature and new extensions that, when combined with the literature profiled in the first book, can provide your students with an array of magical journeys and a host of exciting treasures. It is my hope that you will discover within these pages an infinite variety of creative learning possibilities for your classroom and that your students will discover an exciting cornucopia of mind-expanding, concept-building, and real-world experiences that will reshape their perceptions of what social studies is as well as what it can be. Come aboard and enjoy the ride!

Tony Fredericks

# *Acknowledgments*

This book has been supported, nurtured, and inspired by many people—both individually and collectively.

Thunderous accolades and standing ovations are extended to all my students at York College for their continued dedication and wonderful creativity. The initial impetus for *Social Studies Through Children's Literature: An Integrated Approach* (1991) was generated and promoted in our "Teaching Elementary Social Studies" classes each semester. That same energy and enthusiasm for a literature-based approach to social studies education is carried forward in this new edition. I am continuously inspired by their talent, their ideas, and their sensitivity to the dynamics of a process approach to learning. May their future classrooms be filled with loads of literature and a **plethora** of learning possibilities!

To my daughter Rebecca, who once again has lent her illustrative expertise to another book, goes my love and admiration. May her talents be celebrated and enjoyed for generations to come.

To Erin Sprague, my production editor on this volume, goes a heartfelt thanks for her expertise in masterfully manipulating all the editorial details woven throughout the pages of this book.

To my dog Sienna, a constantly forgiving and uncritical listener to the musings, mumblings, and maledictions of this author, goes my sincerest appreciation and highest accolades. Her place is forever assured beside my computer desk.

# Part I
# Children's Literature in the Social Studies Curriculum

# Chapter 1

## Introduction

## Into the Rainforest

Long arcing lianas hung down from every possible light fixture and corner of the room. An array of greens and golds and reds and blues were splashed across the walls and down the windowpanes. Illustrations of tapirs, harpy eagles, and long-tongued bats and photos of passion-flower butterflies, marmosets, and orchid bees were arrayed throughout the room. The cries of macaws, parrots, and toucans filled the air with a medley of sounds. Occasionally, one heard the flap of wings and distant calls of monkeys. Insects of every size and shape buzzed and whirred as unseen reptiles slithered across the weather-hewn bark of ancient trees. The gurgling of a hidden stream mixed with the animal sounds to create a blend of basses and trebles that ebbed and flowed across the landscape. To any visitor it was evident that this was a place filled with a diversity of life—and an assortment of learning opportunities.

Amy Berenzy has been a fourth-grade teacher in eastern Michigan for the past five years. Visitors entering her classroom often feel as though they have been transported to some lush Amazonian forest. Amy, along with her students, has transformed the room into an ecological wonderland awash in magnificent sights and sounds. This rainforest simulation is so authentic that one might expect an emerald boa to slither from the shadows or, perhaps, a flock of ruby topaz hummingbirds to hover overhead.

Amy knows that most of her students may never have the opportunity to travel to Brazil, or to any other rain-forested country, to experience the sounds and sights of this endangered environment as well as the culture of its indigenous peoples. So, too, does she realize that the rainforests of the world are seriously endangered and that the next generation of children must work together to help preserve the flora and fauna that live in this fragile ecosystem.

So that she could actively involve her students in a host of positive learning experiences, increase their awareness of this geographical region, and offer them hands-on, minds-on activities and projects, Amy presented them with a unit on rainforests. Let's take a few moments and look in on Amy's class as her students explore some of the mysteries and marvels of this magical world.

A group of three girls are comparing notes on information they obtained from back issues of *International Wildlife* and *Wildlife Conservation* about the status of selected endangered species in the rainforests of South America. Hector and Christian have elected to contact various environmental organizations throughout the country (e.g., Rainforest Alliance [270 Lafayette St., Suite 512, New York, NY 10012], Rainforest Action Network [450 Sansome St., Suite 700, San Francisco, CA 94111], Children's Rainforest [P.O. Box 936, Lewiston, ME 04240], and The Nature Conservancy [1815 North Lynn St., Arlington, VA 22209]) to obtain information on each organization's efforts to preserve indigenous peoples. Inez, Diane, Boyd, and Tyrone are working with the school librarian to assemble a bibliography of rainforest literature that can be shared with their pen pals in another fourth-grade class in Detroit.

Darrell, Bruce, and Tran are constructing a terrarium from a plastic soda bottle, soil, pebbles, charcoal, and an assortment of small plants. The terrarium (one of several) will be placed on the window sill and the growth of its life-forms tracked and recorded over several weeks.

Josh, Connie, and Peter are drafting a letter to various political leaders to voice their concerns about the destruction of the rainforest. Maurice and Sharon are replaying a rainforest audiotape, *Costa Rica Soundscapes* (available from The Nature Conservancy, Merchandise Department, P.O. Box 294, Wye Mills, MD 21679 [1-800-382-2386]) and identifying each animal sound. Amanda and Carole are creating a series of posters focusing on representative animals that live in each of the four major layers of the rainforest.

One group of students is preparing to make a short video comparing the rainforests of Africa with those of Brazil. Sandra, Da'nelle, Janet, and Tim are interviewing other fourth-grade students for questions to pose the anthropology professor who will be visiting from the University of Michigan. Abraham and Michael have begun looking through several books to collect information about the life of the Yanomami peoples of the Amazon River basin. Roger and Bobbie are setting up a soil experiment to test the rapid depletion of nutrients from the rainforest during flooding.

Enthusiasm echoes throughout the classroom. Students are excited about sharing information, about discussing ideas for presenting data to other classes, and about deciding how to use their knowledge productively. Some students choose to pursue independent activities, while others work quietly in small groups. Cooperative learning is evident as students assemble ideas and share possibilities in an atmosphere of mutual respect and support. Competition is rare; students help each other with ideas, resources, and extensions of activities. It is apparent that this is a true community of learners in which students work toward common goals, make decisions and follow through on them, and take as much responsibility for *how* they learn as for *what* they learn.

Amy's students are engaged in a series of well-planned and thoroughly engaging learning opportunities wrapped around a variety of children's literature. The unit she designed assists students in learning about specific aspects of life in the rainforest, helps them appreciate the various rainforests of the world, and makes them aware of the anthropological, geographical, and environmental factors of selected rainforests. Amy had introduced the unit with a collection of books about the rainforests, including those dealing with climate, explorations, rates of destruction, medicines obtained from rainforest plants, and some of the most unusual animals found anywhere in the world. Her primary resource was *Exploring the*

*Rainforest: Science Activities for Kids* by Anthony D. Fredericks (Golden, CO: Fulcrum, 1996). Her other resources included *A Walk in the Rainforest* by Kristin Pratt (Nevada City, CA: Dawn Publications, 1992); *Life in the Rainforest* by Lucy Baker (New York: Scholastic, 1990); *Rain Forest* by Barbara Taylor (New York: Dorling Kindersley, 1992); *The Great Kapok Tree* by Lynne Cherry (San Diego, CA: Harcourt Brace Jovanovich, 1990); *Tropical Rain Forests Around the World* by Elaine Landau (New York: Watts, 1991); *Welcome to the Green House* by Jane Yolen (New York: Putnam's, 1993); *Rain Forest Secrets* by Arthur Dorros (New York: Scholastic, 1990); and *Nature's Green Umbrella* by Gail Gibbons (New York: Morrow Junior Books, 1994). Although these books were the impetus for the unit, Amy also offered her students a wide-ranging assortment of hands-on experiences, activities, experiments, and projects that provided engaging and exciting opportunities for learning for several weeks.

Amy's social studies curriculum provides her students with a variety of stimulating activities, a classroom overflowing with books and opportunities to read those books in productive ways, and a program abundant with meaningful social studies activities. In short, Amy facilitates active learning and values the depth and breadth to which students can become immersed in their own academic endeavors.

In Amy's classroom, social studies comes alive and becomes an exciting and dynamic part of everyday classroom activities. Social studies is not separated from other subjects, but is naturally blended into a coherent curriculum that offers opportunities for learning to each student. The obvious advantage is that students see the natural relationships and interrelationships that exist between social studies and other subjects; those subjects are an extension of the social studies program and are equally supported by it.

# Views of Social Studies

In my *Teaching Elementary Social Studies* course, I frequently ask prospective teachers to list their recollections or reactions to their social studies classes when they were elementary students. Following are samples of comments that are typically presented by students:

"It was dull and boring."

"I hated it!"

"All we did was read from the textbook and answer questions at the end of each chapter."

"It was always done at the end of the day for about 20 minutes or so."

"I hated it!"

"The teacher wasn't very excited about teaching it."

"The textbook was out of date and wasn't very interesting."

"I hated it!"

These comments are probably indicative of many students' experiences with social studies. Social studies may be seen by most students as an unmotivating and uninspirational part of the elementary curriculum. It is often relegated to the end of the day or squeezed in when time allows or when teachers are required to address it. As a result, students often believe that social studies is the least important subject in the curriculum simply because it 1) is given the least time compared with subjects such as reading and math; 2) teachers are required to use out-of-date and uninspiring textbooks; 3) a dearth of supplemental materials and projects is available in social studies; and 4) it is often usurped by assemblies, field trips, and other special programs. As a result, students may get the idea that social studies is a filler subject, which can be pulled in and out of the curriculum at will according to the demands of other subjects or at the inclination of the teacher.

In my conversations with teachers around the country, I have also discovered that they, too, frequently show a less-than-enthusiastic response to the social studies program. Perhaps their experiences with social studies when they were students were the result of an overburdened curriculum that allotted less and less time to more and more subjects. As a result, social studies frequently gets short shrift—inserted here and there whenever possible or taught somewhat less enthusiastically than subjects such as reading and language arts. Teachers, just like their students, may feel that social studies textbooks are significantly less stimulating than other texts, but they are required to use them, whether they like to or not. As a result, the social studies program may receive the least amount of attention compared to other subjects, resulting in decreased enthusiasm from both teachers and students.

Indeed, social studies may be the least favorite subject of both teachers and students alike. I suspect that a major reason is that it is viewed as a textbook-bound topic: The information, knowledge, and skills that must be taught and learned come mainly from textbooks. Few opportunities exist for students to take an active role in their own learning and appreciation of social studies, nor are there many opportunities for teachers to provide projects and activities that enhance social studies and make it come alive for their classes. In short, social studies is often treated as a passive subject; much factual information is fed to children with few opportunities for them to process the data actively.

Trying to teach social studies within an overactive and overburdened curriculum may seem daunting to many teachers, yet my own classroom experiences, as well as those of several colleagues, suggest that it need not be so. We have discovered that when good literature for children is integrated fully into the social studies curriculum, children gain opportunities for learning that extend far beyond the pages of the text and that enhance their attitudes and aptitudes *across the curriculum.*

The integration of literature into the social studies curriculum is timely in that a wealth of new and exciting children's books that enhance social studies in intriguing and interesting ways is now being published. A variety of trade books, old and new, adds immeasurably to the entire social studies program. Also, the integration of children's literature into the social studies program is supported by recent curricular changes in several states, each of which has adopted guidelines that underscore a strong relationship between teaching literature and teaching social studies. Even more interesting is that many textbook publishers are now rushing to include literature selections as part of the lessons in their new text series.

*More Social Studies Through Children's Literature* is based on the idea that incorporating trade books into the elementary social studies program provides students with extended opportunities for learning that go far beyond the facts and figures of social studies. New worlds of discovery and exploration open up for students through the magic of literature; these worlds that expand the curriculum and enlarge students' appreciation of their environment and their place in it.

# The Social Studies Curriculum

Social studies is a broad-based exploration of people, how they live, and how people get along with one another. To that end, social studies encompasses all of the other disciplines of the elementary curriculum. For example, reading provides us with the tools to study and learn about people; science gives us opportunities to understand people and their interactions with the environment; language arts allows people to communicate with one another; and math provides us with the quantitative tools to measure and evaluate our world. In short, **social studies is not an isolated subject, but rather one that can and should be integrated throughout all the academic experiences of children**.

The scope and sequence of most social studies programs are based on tradition as well as suggestions from the National Council for the Social Studies (NCSS). Typically, most elementary programs are designed according to the following hierarchy:

- *Child/Self.* At this stage, usually initiated at the kindergarten level, students are given opportunities to investigate topics most familiar to them, including their persons, going to school, rules for safe living, and working together.

- *Families.* Here children are exposed to aspects of what families do, as well as the world beyond that of their own families. Topics at this level may include the relationship of the individual to the family, families and their needs, how families work, and families in neighborhoods.

- *Communities/Neighborhoods.* At this stage of the social studies program, students are introduced to neighborhoods and communities. Typical topics include transportation and communication, community services, celebrating holidays, how neighborhoods change, and rural and urban communities.

- *Cities/Country.* At this level students are exposed to information on larger community concepts. Usually comparisons are made between communities and cities through the parts of a city, life in early cities, local government, comparative cultures, and locations of cities.

- *States/Regions.* This level of the social studies curriculum includes information on different sections of the United States as well as various geographical characteristics of selected states. Emphasis includes comparative studies on deserts, mountains, plains, and forests of the United States (and other selected areas within our country).

- *Nation/United States.* The primary emphasis at this level is on the United States, although it may include reference to Canada and/or Latin America. Topics include the founding of our country, historical facts, geographical data, chronology, and our cultural and ethnic heritage.

- *World.* This level often includes a number of topics dealing with either the Western or Eastern Hemispheres (or both). Areas covered include ancient civilizations, Asia, Europe, Africa, and the Middle East. At this level, the curriculum is crowded and diverse.

The above curriculum is usually referred to as the *widening horizons* or *expanding environments* curriculum. It is based on the idea that children need to deal first with concepts that are relative to their immediate environment (self) and systematically progress to concepts that move in concentric circles out and beyond that environment (see figure 1.1).

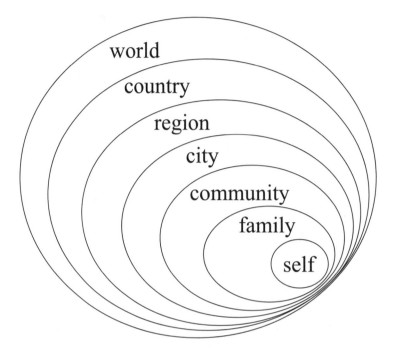

**Fig. 1.1. Systematic progression in the social studies curriculum.**

Although most social studies curricula are predicated on the expanding environments idea, teachers need to be cognizant of the interests, needs, and abilities of their students if they are to present a constantly evolving and dynamic social studies program. In short, good social studies programs allow for modification of the expanding environments plan; they begin with what children know, but they also include content that allows students to venture beyond their immediate environments.

# Rethinking the Social Studies Curriculum

Whether you have been teaching for one year or for 31 years, you undoubtedly hold assumptions, biases, and beliefs about what social studies is and how students learn this all-important subject. After nearly 30 years of teaching, I too, have some ideas and beliefs about teaching in general and teaching social studies in particular. Take a few minutes to review these preconceptions and note how literature can and should be part of the teaching/learning cycle in social studies. You need not agree with every statement, but do evaluate them through your own philosophy of how to teach social studies and how children can learn social studies.

1. The textbook should not be the entire social studies program. Instead, the program should be broad-based, including a variety of materials and learning options.

2. Students have different learning styles, interests, and abilities. The well-rounded curriculum provides opportunities for each student to learn rather than targeting the so-called average student (if there is such a creature).

3. Integrating social studies into the rest of the curriculum can be a positive experience for children. Students should be able to experience a broad definition of social studies as a positive dimension of all the other subject areas.

4. A child-centered curriculum is more meaningful and relevant than a teacher-directed one. When students are provided with opportunities to make their own decisions and select learning activities in keeping with their needs and interests, learning becomes much more productive.

5. Inquiry-based learning has powerful implications in any classroom. Allowing students to chart their own paths of discovery and investigation can lead to the inculcation of valuable concepts.

6. Social studies instruction that relies on the memorization of dates, names, places, facts, and figures is boring! Placing this information in a context that has meaning for students helps them appreciate significant data as it relates to their lives.

7. Social studies should be taught all day, every day. This statement may be difficult to accept for most teachers, yet it is possible to infuse social studies into every aspect of the elementary curriculum without limiting other subjects or running out of time.

8. Teachers do not need to be repositories of all there is to know about social studies. When teachers work with their students to investigate and learn about areas of mutual interest, children receive a powerful message that one person does not need to know every fact and figure to be competent in social studies. Instead, individuals should be willing to share knowledge and information in mutually supportive ways.

9. Social studies is just as important as reading, math, science, and language arts! Social studies becomes important in children's lives when it is integrated into their life experiences and is used to extend those experiences.

10. Social studies is fun! Social studies can be one of the most dynamic, exciting, stimulating, and invigorating elements of any school day—particularly when it is taught by an enthusiastic teacher!

# The Literature-Based Approach to Social Studies Instruction

Many social studies programs are designed to *give* children lots of information, have them *memorize* that data, and then ask them to *recall* the information on various assessment instruments. As discussed earlier, this may be a significant reason for students' less than enthusiastic response to social studies. That type of instruction does not allow students active involvement in their own learning, nor does it allow children opportunities to think creatively about what they are learning.

My own experiences as a teacher have taught me that when students, no matter what their abilities or interests, are provided with opportunities to manipulate information in productive ways, learning becomes much more meaningful. I refer to this as a *process approach to learning* because it provides an abundance of projects, activities, and instructional designs and allows students to make decisions and solve problems. In so doing, students sense that learning is much more than memorizing facts. Rather, what children do with that knowledge determines its impact on their attitudes and aptitudes.

A process approach to social studies allows children to *do* something with the concepts and generalizations they learn. It implies that students can manipulate, decide, solve, predict, and structure the knowledge of social studies in ways that are meaningful to them. When teachers provide opportunities for students to process information actively, learning becomes more child-centered and less text-based. This results in an expansive, integrated, and dynamic social studies program.

A literature-based approach to social studies is a combination of activities, children's literature, hands-on, minds-on projects, and materials used to expand a social studies concept or idea. Literature-based social studies teaching and learning is multidisciplinary and multidimensional: It knows no boundaries and has no limits. A literature-based approach to social studies offers students a realistic arena in which they can learn and investigate social studies concepts for extended periods. It is a process approach to learning of the highest magnitude.

This approach to social studies instruction is built on the idea that learning can be integrative and multifaceted. A literature-based approach to social studies education provides children with a host of opportunities to become actively involved in the dynamics of their own learning and to draw positive relationships between what happens inside and outside the classroom. Literature-based teaching promotes social studies education as a sustaining and relevant venture.

## Social Studies Teaching and Multiple Intelligences

Literature-based instruction in social studies offers a host of opportunities for students to participate in a constructivist approach to learning. It provides a variety of meaningful learning opportunities tailored to students' needs and interests. Children are given the chance to make important choices about *what* they learn as well as about *how* they learn. Literature-based instruction provides the means to integrate the social studies program with the rest of the elementary curriculum while involving students in a multiplicity of learning opportunities and ventures.

Opportunities for students to hone, build, and take advantage of one or more of their multiple intelligences are incorporated into literature-based explorations. According to Howard Gardner *(Frames of Mind: The Theory of Multiple Intelligences*. New York: Basic Books, HarperCollins, 1985), each individual possesses eight different intelligences in varying degrees. These intelligences (as opposed to a single intelligence quotient as traditionally reported via many standardized intelligence tests) help determine how individuals learn and how they fare in their daily lives. Gardner defines an *intelligence* as consisting of three components:

- The ability to create an effective product or offer a service that is valuable in one's culture.

- A set of skills that enables an individual to solve problems encountered in life.

- The potential for finding or creating solutions for problems, which enables a person to acquire new knowledge.

Individuals differ in the strength (or weakness) of each of the eight intelligences in isolation as well as in combination. For example, whereas some individuals learn best through linguistic means, others are more kinesthetic learners, and still others are spatial learners. Suffice to say that no two people learn in the same way, nor should they be taught in the same way (see figure 1.2).

---

# The Eight Human Intelligences

1. *Verbal-Linguistic Intelligence* involves ease in producing language and sensitivity to the nuances, order, and rhythm of words. Individuals who are strong in verbal-linguistic intelligence love to read, write, and tell stories.

   Enhancement Activities: Writing, reading, storytelling, speaking, debating

2. *Logical-Mathematical Intelligence* relates to the ability to reason deductively or inductively and to recognize and manipulate abstract patterns and relationships. Individuals who excel in this intelligence have strong problem-solving and reasoning skills and ask questions in a logical manner.

   Enhancement Activities: Problem solving, outlining, calculating, patterning, showing relationships

3. *Musical-Rhythmic Intelligence* encompasses sensitivity to the pitch, timbre, and rhythm of sounds as well as responsiveness to the emotional implications of these elements of music. Individuals who remember melodies or recognize pitch and rhythm exhibit musical intelligence.

   Enhancement Activities: Composing, singing, humming, making instrumental sounds, creating vibrations

4. *Visual-Spatial Intelligence* includes the ability to create visual-spatial representations of the world and to transfer them mentally or concretely. Individuals who exhibit spatial intelligence need a mental or physical picture to best understand new information. They are strong in drawing, designing, and creating things.

   Enhancement Activities: Painting, drawing, sculpting, pretending, imagining

5. *Bodily-Kinesthetic Intelligence* involves using the body to solve problems, make things, and convey ideas and emotions. Individuals who are strong in this intelligence are good at physical activities, eye-hand coordination, and have a tendency to move around, touch things, and gesture.

   Enhancement Activities: Dancing, miming, role playing, exercising, playing games

6. *Intrapersonal Intelligence* entails the ability to understand one's own emotions, goals, and intentions. Individuals strong in intrapersonal intelligence have strong sense of self, are confident, and can enjoy working alone.

   Enhancement Activities: Thinking strategies, focusing, metacognitive techniques, silent reflection, emotional processing

7. *Interpersonal Intelligence* refers to the ability to work effectively with other people and to understand them and recognize their goals and intentions. Individuals who exhibit this intelligence thrive on cooperative work, have strong leadership skills, and are skilled at organizing, communicating, and negotiating.

   Enhancement Activities: Communicating, receiving feedback, collaborating, cooperating, structured feedback

8. *Naturalist Intelligence* includes the capacity to recognize flora and fauna; to make distinctions in the natural world; and to use this ability productively in activities such as farming and biological science.

   Enhancement Activities: Planting, raising and tending, nurturing, observing, experimenting.

**Fig. 1.2. The eight human intelligences.**

Research on multiple intelligences has revealed that teaching aimed at sharpening one kind of intelligence will carry over to others. Mounting evidence shows that learning opportunities involving a variety of intelligences allow students to take advantage of their preferred intelligence(s) and to strengthen their weaker intelligences.

Literature-based instruction provides something for everyone. It allows you to extend, expand, and take advantage of students' intelligences. Literature-based instruction also provides you with opportunities to combine the intelligences of your students with the resources, information, and scientific principles of your entire social studies curriculum. **Literature-based teaching celebrates *multiple* intelligences; it provides learning opportunities that give students a meaningful and balanced approach to social studies learning.** Above all, literature-based instruction supports and emphasizes the varied relationships that exist among social studies inquiry, a process approach to learning, and the exercise of multiple intelligences in a positive and supportive environment.

# Advantages of Literature-Based Instruction

Literature-based instruction in social studies offers a plethora of advantages for both teachers and students (see figure 1.3).

## Advantages of Literature-Based Instruction

- Emphasizes and celebrates an individual's multiple intelligences in a supportive and creative learning environment.

- Focuses on the *processes* of social studies rather than the *products* of social studies.

- Reduces and/or eliminates the artificial barriers that often exist between curricular areas and provides an integrative approach to learning.

- Promotes a child-centered social studies curriculum—one in which they are encouraged to make their own decisions and assume a measure of responsibility for learning.

- Stimulates self-directed discovery and investigation both in and out of the classroom.

- Assists youngsters in developing relationships between social studies ideas and concepts, thus enhancing appreciation and comprehension.

- Stimulates the creation of important social studies concepts through first-hand experiences and self-initiated discoveries.

- More time is available for instructional purposes. Social studies instruction does not *have* to be crammed into limited, artificial time periods, but can be extended across the curriculum and throughout the day.

- The connections that can and do exist between social studies and other subjects, topics, and themes can be logically and naturally developed. Teachers can demonstrate relationships and assist students in comprehending those relationships.

- Social studies can be promoted as a continuous activity—one not restricted by textbook designs, time barriers, or even the four walls of the classroom. Teachers can help students extend social studies learning into many aspects of their personal lives.

- Teachers are free to help students look at a social studies problem, situation, or topic from a variety of viewpoints, as opposed to their viewing it "the right way," frequently demonstrated in a teacher's manual or curriculum guide.

- Teachers can place more emphasis on *teaching* students and less on *telling* students.

- Teachers can promote problem solving, creative thinking, and critical thinking within all dimensions of a topic.

**Fig. 1.3. Advantages of literature-based instruction.**

Traditional approaches to social studies instruction rely primarily on packaged materials, usually in the form of commercial social studies series and the ubiquitous teacher's manual and student textbooks. A major disadvantage is that students often perceive social studies as textbook-based or as taking place at a certain time in the school day. Literature-based instruction in social studies, however, provides students (and teachers) with an expanded curriculum that has no limits or boundaries. Compare some of the differences between literature-based instruction in social studies and more traditional forms of classroom organization such as textbooks and school/district curriculum guides (see table 1.1).

**Table 1.1. Comparison of Literature-Based and Text-Based Curricula**

| *LITERATURE-BASED INSTRUCTION* | *TEXTBOOK-BASED LEARNING* |
|---|---|
| Gives students a sense of ownership of their learning. | Teacher makes all decisions as to what will be learned and when. |
| Facilitates responsible learning. | Students are told what to do, but not always why. |
| Is holistic in nature. | Is fragmented and disconnected. |
| Encourages risk taking. | Emphasizes the accumulation of "right" answers. |
| Promotes inquiry and reflection. | Teacher asks most of the questions and has most of the answers. |
| Breaks down artificial curricular boundaries; integrates the entire curriculum. | Segmented and divided curriculum is imposed. |
| Encourages collaborative and cooperative learning. | Students attempt to get high marks or good grades (vis-à-vis tests and exams). |
| Has teacher model appropriate learning behaviors. | Teacher dictates learning behaviors. |
| Uses assessment that is authentic, meaningful, and infused throughout the learning process. | Assessment occurs at the end of learning a predetermined body of knowledge and is teacher-controlled. |
| Encourages self-direction and individual inquiries. | Everyone must learn the same body of knowledge. |
| Helps students understand the WHY of what they're learning. | Students are told what to learn. |
| Allows students to make approximations of learning. | Students must learn absolutes. |
| Promotes, supports, and stimulates multiple intelligences. | Everyone learns through a formal, standardized lecture/recitation process. |

Literature-based instruction facilitates the teaching of social studies as much as it does the learning of social studies. It broadens and strengthens the entire social studies curriculum, which, in turn, becomes more attentive to the development of individual social studies competencies.

# Chapter 2

## *Making Connections*

Children's literature in the social studies curriculum should be a natural and normal part of students' experiences with social studies. It provides youngsters with valuable opportunities to extend and expand their knowledge of the world around them as well as to develop a rich appreciation for the social studies concepts, values, and generalizations contained within good literature. By infusing books and literature into your social studies program, you are helping students understand that social studies is much more than a dry accumulation of facts and dates. Instead, you are helping your students explore and investigate their immediate and far-flung world in an arena that knows no limits.

The use of literature within social studies is based on several precepts:

1. Literature provides an ever-expanding array of information in a welcome and familiar format to students.

2. Literature extends the social studies curriculum beyond any textbook constraints.

3. Literature relates to children's lives in diverse and divergent ways.

4. Literature, both fiction and nonfiction, helps children understand their cultural, ethnic, and religious heritage.

5. Literature assists children in developing positive attitudes towards themselves, people in their immediate environment, and peoples from around the world.

6. Literature provides vicarious *and* first-hand experiences with all social studies disciplines.

7. Literature provides students with new information and knowledge unobtainable in any other format.

8. Literature stimulates creative thinking and problem-solving abilities in a variety of contexts.

9.  Literature opens up the world and draws students in to make self-initiated discoveries.

10. Literature is fun!

When high-quality literature is made a significant part of the social studies program, children can become involved in activities and gain experiences they may not be exposed to within a text-based program.

# The National Council for the Social Studies Standards

In response to a demand for a cohesive set of standards that addresses overall curriculum design and comprehensive student performance expectations in social studies education, the National Council for the Social Studies developed and promulgated the NCSS Standards. These standards are organized around broad themes and provide a focused outline of the essential components of a well-structured social studies curriculum.

Not only do the standards provide an outline for the development of social studies instruction, they also bring coordination, consistency, and coherence to the improvement of social studies education. As such, the standards represent 10 basic themes:

Culture

Time, Continuity, and Change

People, Places, and Environment

Individual Development and Identity

Individuals, Groups, and Institutions

Power, Authority, and Governance

Production, Distribution, and Consumption

Science, Technology, and Society

Global Connections

Civic Ideals and Practices

The NCSS Standards (see figure 2.1) are intentionally integrative and multidisciplinary. That is, several traditional social studies disciplines (sociology, history, political science, geography, anthropology, and economics) may be blended to form a more cohesive look at a topic or theme. This does not diminish the import of those disciplines, but rather provides classroom teachers with a plethora of extended teaching and learning opportunities throughout the entire social studies curriculum.

# Social Studies Standards (Abridged)

## I. Culture

The study of culture prepares students to answer questions such as: What are the common characteristics of different cultures? How do belief systems, such as religion and political ideals, influence other parts of the culture? What does language tell us about the culture? Relevant courses and disciplines include geography, history, sociology, and anthropology.

## II. Time, Continuity, and Change

Human beings seek to understand their historical roots and to locate themselves in time. Knowing how to reconstruct the past allows one to develop a historical perspective and to answer questions such as: What happened in the past? How has the world changed? How will the world change in the future? Relevant courses and disciplines include history.

## III. People, Places, and Environment

The study of people, places, and human-environment interactions assists students as they create their views and geographic perspectives of the world. Students need to answer questions such as: Where are things located? Why are they located where they are? How do landforms change? Relevant courses and disciplines include geography and areas studies.

## IV. Individual Development and Identity

Personal identity is shaped by one's culture, by groups, and by institutional influences. Students consider such questions as: How do people learn? Why do people behave as they do? How do people meet their basic needs? How do individuals develop from youth to adulthood? Relevant courses and disciplines include psychology and anthropology.

## V. Individuals, Groups, and Institutions

Institutions such as schools, churches, families, government agencies, and the courts play an integral role in people's lives. It is important that students learn how institutions are formed, what controls and influences them, and how they are maintained or changed. Students may address questions such as: What is the role of institutions in this and other societies? How am I influenced by institutions? What is my role in institutional change? Relevant courses and disciplines include sociology, anthropology, psychology, political science, and history.

*(continued on p. 20)*

## VI. Power, Authority, and Governance

Understanding the structures of power, authority, and governance and their evolving functions in contemporary U.S. society and other parts of the world is essential for developing civic competence. Students need to confront questions such as: What is power? How is it gained? How can individual rights be protected? Relevant courses and disciplines include government, politics, political science, history, law, and other social sciences.

## VII. Production, Distribution, and Consumption

Because people have wants that often exceed the resources available to them, a variety of ways have evolved to answer such questions as: What is to be produced? How is production organized? How are goods and services to be distributed? Relevant courses and disciplines include economics.

## VIII. Science, Technology, and Society

Modern life as we know it would not be possible without technology and the science that supports it. But technology brings with it many questions such as: Is new technology better than old? How can we cope with the pace of technology? How can we manage technology so that the greatest number of people benefit from it? Relevant courses and disciplines include history, geography, economics, civics, and government.

## IX. Global Connections

The realities of global interdependence require understanding the increasingly important and diverse global connections among world societies. Students need to address such international issues as health care, the environment, human rights, economic competition, and political alliances. Relevant courses and disciplines include geography, culture, and economics. This theme may also draw upon the natural and physical sciences and the humanities.

## X. Civic Ideals and Practices

An understanding of civic ideals and practices of citizenship is critical to full participation in society. Students confront such questions as: What is civic participation and how can I be involved? What is the balance between rights and responsibilities? What is the role of the citizen in the community? Relevant courses and disciplines include history, political science, cultural anthropology, and fields such as global studies, law-related education, and the humanities.

**Fig. 2.1. The NCSS Standards**

Author abridgement from the Executive Summary of *Expect Excellence:
Curriculum Standards for Social Studies Electronic Edition* (1996). 2–4.

In reviewing the standards above, you will notice that their many elements can be promoted in the philosophy and design of a literature-based approach to social studies education. That the standards assist teachers in defining the structural components of an effective social studies unit and the environment in which that instruction can take place is equally important. The following description illustrates how one teacher integrated the standards into an extended lesson plan.

# A Sample Teaching Plan

Megan Armbruster is a fourth-grade teacher in Southern California. With almost 10 years of teaching experience she has been a long-time advocate of literature-based instruction, particularly in social studies. In addition, she also believes that the NCSS Standards have helped her create an environment for learning in which she and her students can work together as active learners. Her social studies program is based on four assumptions: 1) a successful social studies curriculum is never static; 2) social studies instruction can be extended throughout the curriculum; 3) teachers should facilitate rather than lecture; and 4) students' understanding of social studies concepts is actively constructed through a variety of individual and social processes.

Following is a single-day lesson plan Megan used as part of a three-week unit on *Communities*. Each of the activities has been coded to one or more of the NCSS Standards for Social Studies.

# Unit: Communities

(Day #6—Transportation)

**8:30–8:50 OPENING**

After putting away their book bags, students assemble around a table on which are several different daily newspapers (e.g., *San Francisco Chronicle, Los Angeles Times, New York Times*). Students are invited to look through the newspapers for articles regarding different forms of transportation (transit system, car advertisements, bicycle sale, etc.). They cut out selected articles and assemble them into an ongoing journal. One small group of students is creating a dictionary booklet entitled *Our Transportation Book*. They reserve a page for each letter of the alphabet (e.g., A = Automobile; B = Bicycle; C = Carriage; D = Diving Bell). **[Standards I, III, VII]**

**8:50–9:15 WHOLE-CLASS INSTRUCTION**

Megan shows *Transportation* (video, National Geographic Society, Washington, D.C.; Catalog No. A51492) [This film explains how transportation systems link a community, move its goods, and connect it with the rest of the world]. Afterwards, she takes the students outside and to the front of the school. She invites small groups of students to record the various forms of transportation that pass the school during a designated period (15 minutes). Upon returning to the classroom, she invites students to construct bar graphs of the different vehicles observed. She plans time to talk with students about any inferences they have made about the community based solely on the types of vehicles they observed in their small part of that community. **[Standards I, V]**

## 9:15–9:45 WRITING PROCESS

*Facts on File.* A group of students goes to the school library to research the inventions of various forms of transportation. They collect information about the time and place of each invention and how it contributed to society in general.

*Journals.* Several students take charge of monitoring the events surrounding modifications in the local bus system as reported in the local newspaper. After recording the events in their journals, the students compare their individual interpretations of those events.

*Newspaper.* A small group of students design a weekly newspaper that reports transportation accidents from around the world. Each event is assigned a reporter and is developed into an article.

*Interviews.* Several students initiate a series of interviews with graduate students and professors at UCLA. The interviews center upon an urban planning course and the implications of the course's concepts for a specific community. **[Standards II, III, V, VIII]**

## 9:45–10:30 DRAMA TIME

Students have been divided into four separate groups. Each group constructs a salt map town on a sheet of plywood, each of which employs a single form of municipal transportation (e.g., buses, subway, monorail, etc.). When the students have completed the towns, along with the requisite commercial and residential buildings, they create dramatizations based upon each type of transportation system (e.g., problems encountered, city council meetings, newspaper editorials, etc.) and their effects on the imaginary towns. Students are invited to make videotapes of their skits. **[Standards VI, X]**

## 10:30–11:30 REQUIRED/OPTIONAL ACTIVITIES

*Group 1.* Under the direction of the teacher's aide, students invent a new form of urban transportation designed to move people rapidly and efficiently.

*Group 2.* Students use the Internet (**http://www.askanexpert.com/askanexpert**) to contact various transportation experts and request information on the benefits of different types of mass transit systems. The data will be collected in the form of charts and graphs.

*Group 3.* Students erect a "graffiti wall" outside the classroom and invite students from other classes to record personal information or thoughts about transportation. Later, these ideas will be reconstructed in the form of a giant semantic web.

*Group 4.* After reading *My Family Vacation* by Dayal Khalsa (New York: Crown, 1988), students are composing a book of adjectives and descriptive phrases that have described various forms of transportation used in the United States.

*Group 5.* Students have obtained the address of the U.S. Department of Commerce. They are writing to request the descriptive brochures and information on the role of that agency in establishing regulations regarding oceanic transportation. The data will be compared with information collected from various library resources and newspaper clippings. **[Standards III, V, VI, VIII, X]**

**11:30–12:00 LUNCH**

**12:00–12:30 SUSTAINED SILENT READING**

Students obtain books from the collection offered by Megan and disperse throughout the room. Books selected include *Trains* by Gail Gibbons (New York: Holiday House, 1987); *Trucks* by Gail Gibbons (New York: Thomas Y. Crowell, 1981); *I Go with My Family to Grandma's* by Riki Levinson (New York: Dutton, 1986); and *Up in the Air* by Myra Cohn Livingston (New York: Holiday House, 1989). Several groups of two and three students share their selected books in cooperative reading groups. **[Standards IV, X]**

**12:30–1:15 TEACHER-DIRECTED ACTIVITIES**

*Opening.* Megan decides to open the day's lesson with an *Anticipation Guide*. Using *Ruby* by Michael Emberley (Boston: Little, Brown, 1990), she has created a set of statements (see table 2.1), which she presents to her students before they read the book.

**Table 2.1. Anticipation Guide**

| BEFORE | AFTER | |
|--------|-------|---|
| _____ | _____ | 1. Taxis operate only in cities. |
| _____ | _____ | 2. Buses are a form of municipal transportation. |
| _____ | _____ | 3. Walking in cities is always dangerous. |
| _____ | _____ | 4. Cars are a problem in large cities. |
| _____ | _____ | 5. There are many different ways of traveling in a city. |

Megan gives each student a duplicated copy of the Anticipation Guide and invites everyone to record *True* or *False* in the BEFORE column, depending on his or her beliefs.

*Class Discussion.* The class discusses the responses made on individual anticipation guides. Students voice agreements and disagreements and record their ideas on a special area of the chalkboard. Megan invites students to make predictions about the book.

*Selected Reading.* Megan reads *Ruby* to the class. Before doing so, she invites students to listen for statements or information that may confirm or modify their responses to the anticipation guide statements recorded earlier. She also stops periodically throughout the reading to invite students to change or alter their original predictions based on data in the book.

*Closure.* Megan invites students to assemble in small groups and complete the AFTER column of the anticipation guide (based on the information learned in the book, students record *True* or *False* in the space before each statement). Later, she encourages students to share reasons for their responses and any changes they may have made in their original recordings. Megan encourages students to confirm their ideas through reading more literature. **[Standards I, III, IV, X]**

## 1:15–1:35 STORYTELLING/READ-ALOUD

The students gather on the large reading rug at the back of the classroom to listen to Megan read from *Just Us Women* by Jeanette Caines (New York: Harper & Row, 1982). Afterwards, students discuss vacations they have taken with their families. The various forms of transportation used in those vacations as well as alternate modes of transportation that could have been used are central to the discussion. **[Standards III, IV]**

## 1:35–2:10 ART/MUSIC

The art teacher, Miss McMillan, has posted a large sheet of newsprint in the school cafeteria. Students, in small groups, create a large mural of different modes of transportation used in selected countries around the world. Miss McMillan has shared slides of Diego Rivera's murals, which have been painted on public buildings throughout Mexico (she plans to extend this lesson into a series of geography and history lessons on the land and culture of Mexico). **[Standard IX]**

## 2:10–2:40 SELF-SELECTED ACTIVITIES

*Group 1.* A small group of students prepares a series of travel brochures to cultural and artistic venues in and around Southern California. They accent the various forms of transportation (excluding the family car) that goes to those sites.

*Group 2.* Students contact the owners and managers of selected businesses to request information on how they ship their products and goods. The students then construct a descriptive poster illustrating all the forms of transportation used.

*Group 3.* Students create an extended time line of the major events in transportation history (invention of the wheel, invention of the locomotive, invention of the helicopter, invention of the space shuttle). They post the time line in the school library.

*Group 4.* Students write letters to university students at the University of California—Irvine to request a personal visit. They invite the college students to share information on the effects of technology in the development of new forms of transportation throughout history.

*Group 5.* Two small groups of students each compile bibliographies of current trade books related to transportation in the twentieth century. They will share the bibliographies with teachers in other classes. **[Standards II, III, V, VIII, X]**

## 2:40–3:00 RESPONDING TO LITERATURE

Students finish reading *Mailing May* by Michael O. Tunnell (New York: Greenwillow Books, 1997). The class separates into three groups. The first group discusses the similarities between transportation systems in the early part of the twentieth century and those of today. A second group develops a *story map*, which outlines the major elements of the book in a graphic representation. The third group summarizes the major points of the book in the form of a newspaper article to be included in the class newspaper, *Transportation Watch*. **[Standards II, III]**

**3:00–3:15 DAILY CLOSURE**

The class divides into teams of three students each. The teams discuss some of the items they have learned during the day, items remaining for them to work on in following days, and those items for which they would still like to obtain additional information. Each team's recorder shares some of the discussion with the entire class. Megan invites the students to share their ideas with their parents. **[Standards IV]**

**3:15 DISMISSAL**

# Changing Social Studies Instruction

Megan and thousands of other teachers around the country have discovered that the NCSS Standards and literature-based instruction in social studies are both mutually supportive and, most important, offer classroom teachers multiple opportunities to share the joy and excitement of social studies education with greater numbers of students. This marriage facilitates social studies instruction (particularly for those who have had less-than-pleasurable experiences in their own educational background) and helps students view social studies as a process of discovery and exploration, rather than one of memorization and regurgitation.

Megan knows that the standards, in concert with high-quality trade books, are generating remarkable changes in her methods of teaching social studies and in how her students learn. Literature-based instruction not only offers students unique opportunities to process and practice hands-on, minds-on social studies, but also provides teachers with integrative strategies and activities that enhance and promote social studies concepts in all curricular areas. In addition, students are assisted in drawing realistic parallels between classroom enterprises and events and circumstances outside the classroom. In short, literature-based instruction in concert with the NCSS Standards can aid students in understanding the relevancy of social studies to their everyday lives—certainly a major goal in any social studies curriculum.

# Chapter 3

## How to Use This Book

Welcome aboard! The following chapters contain a host of activities and processes designated for some of the best trade books in elementary social studies. These books have been selected because of their appropriateness to the social studies curriculum, their adaptability to all grades (K–6) and ability ranges (high–low), and their usefulness in promoting relevant concepts of social studies. Included are Caldecott Award winners and Caldecott Honor Books, Reading Rainbow selections, American Book Award medalists, and classics recommended by teachers and children's librarians throughout the country. In short, there's something for everyone!

The literature selections have been organized around the seven major areas of the elementary social studies curriculum: *self/child, family, community/neighborhood, city/country, states/regions, nation/country,* and *world.* The placement of a book within one of those categories may be arbitrary at best. I attempted to demonstrate the wide variety of children's literature available for every aspect of the social studies program—not to designate a particular book exclusively for a single division. Undoubtedly, you will discover that most of these books can be used across the length and breadth of the social studies curriculum.

The literature included within this book reflects a range of reading levels. You should feel free to select and use literature that best meets the needs and abilities of your students in addition to promoting specific social studies concepts. An energized social studies curriculum includes literature selections throughout. By using the literature presented in these pages, you will discover innumerable opportunities for developing, expanding, and teaching all the social studies standards. In that regard, remember that the readability or difficulty level of a single book should not determine if or how it will be used; rather, the emphasis should be on whether students are interested and motivated to pursue literature-related activities that promote learning in a supportive and holistic social studies curriculum.

Each book includes a host of potential activities and processes. You need not use all those activities. Rather, you and your students should decide on those that best serve the social studies program and your students themselves. Undoubtedly, you will discover activities that you can present to individual students, to small groups, to large groups, or to a class. Providing students with opportunities to select activities within the context of a work of literature can be a powerful and energizing component of your program. When youngsters receive those opportunities, their appreciation of social studies and their interest in learning important social studies concepts grows tremendously.

As students become involved with the various trade books and their accompanying activities, I suggest that you guide them in researching and/or developing other activities based on classroom dynamics and teaching and learning styles. If learning is to have meaning, it must have relevance. I encourage you and your students to make these activities your own. Add to them, adapt them, and allow students to help you design additional activities, extensions, and projects that will challenge them, arouse their natural curiosity, and create a dynamic environment for learning.

# Implementing a Literature-Based Program

Teaching social studies via trade books is not necessarily an all-or-nothing proposition. That is, you need not use a single trade book for a full lesson or full day. It does mean that you have several options as to how you present a book or series of books to your class, how much you want them to dominate your daily curriculum, and how involved you and your students want to be. Obviously, your level of comfort with literature-based teaching and the scope and sequence of your classroom or district social studies curriculum may determine the degree to which you use these books. Here are some options for you to consider:

1. Introduce a single book and provide students with a variety of selected activities (for that book) for one day.

2. Teach a unit built upon a combination of several related books.

3. Design a thematic unit based upon selected pieces of literature within a specific social studies standard (e.g., Culture, People, Places, and Environment, Global Connections).

4. Design a thematic unit based upon selected pieces of literature within a specific social studies discipline (e.g., History, Geography, Political Science).

5. Design a thematic unit based upon selected pieces of literature within a specific social studies concept area (e.g., Families, City and Country, States and Regions).

6. Use the activities for one or two books during an entire day and follow up with the regular curriculum in succeeding days.

7. Use a book or series of books as a follow-up to information and data presented in a textbook or curriculum guide.

8. Provide students with literature-related activities as independent work upon their completing lessons in the regular textbook.

9.  Teach cooperatively with a colleague and present a self-designed thematic unit to both classes at the same time (do this with two classes at the same grade or with two different classes, each at a different grade level).

10. Use a book or group of books intermittently for several weeks.

How you use these books may be determined by any number of factors; there is no ideal way to integrate literature into your classroom plans. The list above is only a partial collection of ideas; the dictates of your own teaching situation, your personal experience, and your students' needs may suggest other possibilities.

*Note*: Throughout this book, I have suggested various Web sites as positive learning extensions of your overall social studies program and for specific trade books. As you know, the Internet is dynamic and constantly changing. The Web sites listed were current and accurate as of the writing of this book. Please be aware that some may change and others may be eliminated; new sites will be added to the various search engines that you use at school or home. If you discover a dead site or a new Web site that other teachers might enjoy, please feel free to contact me at **afrederi@gte.net** or via my own Web site at **http://www.afredericks.com**.

# Part II
## Activities and Processes

# Chapter 4

## Child and Self

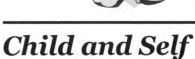

## Amazing Grace
**Mary Hoffman**
(New York: Dial Books for Young Readers, 1991)

### Summary

Grace loves stories—but she especially loves to act out stories. When there's an opportunity to play a part in the school play, *Peter Pan,* Grace wants to be the lead character. Everyone tells her she can't; but with the loving support of her mother and wise grandmother, Grace learns that she can be anything she wants to be, and the results are amazing. This book wonderfully celebrates the human spirit and is a "must have" for any classroom and any child.

### Social Studies Disciplines

sociology

### NCSS Thematic Strands

individual development and identity; individuals, groups, and institutions

### Critical Thinking Questions

1. Does Grace's grandmother remind you of anyone in your family? Would you like to have Grace's grandmother in your family?

2. What did you enjoy most about Grace?

3. Have you ever wanted to do something that other people thought you couldn't do?

4. Would you want Grace as your friend? Why?

**33**

5. If you could be any character from any book, who would you be?

6. What do you think is the most important lesson in this book?

## Related Books

Bowen, Connie. *I Believe in Me*. New York: Unity, 1995.

Heath, Amy. *Sofie's Role*. New York: Four Winds Press, 1992.

Mitchell, Rita. *Hue Boy*. New York: Dial Books for Young Readers, 1993.

Moss, Marissa. *But Not Kate*. New York: Lothrop, Lee & Shepard, 1992.

Nash, Alissa. *Markita*. New York: African American Images, 1997.

Parsons, Alexandra. *I Am Special*. New York: Watts, 1997.

## Activities

1. Since its publication, this book has won numerous awards from various groups and organizations around the country. Invite your students to create and develop their own special award for this book. What qualities or features make it so outstanding? Encourage students to create a fictitious organization (e.g., *The American Self-Esteem Society*) and design an appropriate award. They may wish to hold another the role of the illustrator, another the role of the publisher, etc.).

2. As a read-aloud book, share *Peter Pan* with your students. Invite them to discuss any similarities between *Peter Pan* and *Amazing Grace*. What personal qualities does each book emphasize?

3. Invite students to share and discuss some of the feelings Grace may have experienced. Encourage youngsters to share incidents from their own lives in which they were told they weren't capable of doing something, even though they really wanted to. Plan time to discuss gender (Grace was told she couldn't play Peter Pan because she was a girl.) as well as race (Grace was told that she couldn't play Peter Pan because she was black.). Ensure a comfortable environment for discussion and provide opportunities for students to share their feelings and to respect those of others.

4. Invite each child to create a portrait of himself or herself in the role of a well-known character from a popular book. What characters do they choose? What traits make the character an appropriate choice? Plan time for students to post their characters and discuss their selections.

5. Grace assumes the roles of many book characters: Joan of Arc, Anansi the Spider, adventurer, pirate, Hiawatha, Mowgli, and Aladdin. As part of your daily read-aloud sessions with students, plan opportunities to share some of those books with your students. You may wish to take time after each reading to discuss the personal attributes of each character and why each character is so memorable. Which characteristics are similar to Grace's? Which characteristics are similar to those of individual classmates?

6. Provide students with a variety of old clothes and other props and invite them to dress up (as did Grace) and create their own interpretations of favorite books and stories. Plan opportunities for students to make role reversals (e.g., boys in the roles of female characters; black students in the roles of white characters, etc.). Discuss students' feelings about portraying role-reversed parts.

7. Invite your students to visit another classroom (of the same grade or a grade lower than yours). There, each student can pair with another student to discuss the concept of their being anything they want to be. What can your students tell other students about self-concept and its importance in daily living? Students may wish to precede these discussions with a reading (or acting out) of *Amazing Grace*.

8. Invite students to record important events from their own lives, one event on each of several index cards. Hang some strings along one wall of the classroom or overhead. Provide students with several clothespins and ask each one to select a string and hang his or her cards along the string in their sequential order. Provide opportunities for each student to describe her or his personal time line.

9. Encourage students to interview their parents and other relatives about some of their recollections of memorable events in the student's life. Students may be interested in obtaining more than one retelling about a single event to determine whether different people remember it in the same way. When they have completed the interviews, students may wish to combine their data into an extended directory of important events in their lives.

10. Invite students to create a series of true or false questions about themselves. Print these statements on sheets of paper and duplicate. Pass out one sheet each day and invite students to see how much they know about their classmates. When a sheet is completed, the designated person can stand and explain each of the statements on her or his sheet to the class.

11. Encourage students to write a sequel to *Amazing Grace* from the perspective of the original narrator or from that of Grace herself. They could also write the sequel from the perspective of Grace's class (one or more students) and their newfound perceptions of this remarkable girl.

12. Share several newspaper advertisements (classified ads or display ads) with your students. Invite each student to create an original newspaper ad about herself or himself (as though they were items for sale). Which qualities about themselves do they choose to emphasize in a limited amount of space? Which of their special features might others appreciate (or should appreciate)? Plan time to talk about the characteristics (e.g., personal, physical, etc.) they want to emphasize. Students may wish to gather the completed ads into a classroom newspaper and distribute it around the school.

13. One of the most dynamic theatrical productions for youngsters is readers theatre, an activity in which students read from a prepared script. The emphasis is not on memorization, but rather on each actor's interpretation and presentation of a role. It is a participatory event that helps develop and enhance self-concept. Youngsters gain opportunities to develop self-confidence and self-assurance that may not be available in more traditional class productions.

Your students may enjoy acting in their own theatrical production. The following readers theatre script allows for several interpretations and styles of presentation.

# *Goldilocks and the Three Hamsters*

## *Staging*

The narrator sits off to the side on a tall stool or chair. The other characters can be standing or sitting in chairs (see figure 4.1).

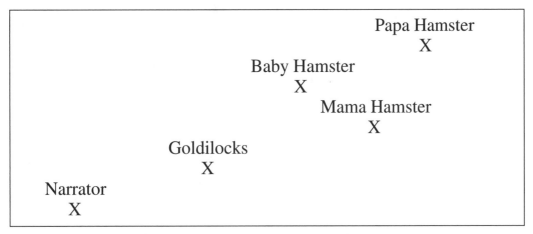

**Fig. 4.1. Staging for *Goldilocks and the Three Hamsters*.**

**Narrator:** Once upon a time there were three hamsters. One was Baby Hamster. He was the smallest. The middle-sized hamster was Mama Hamster. The biggest hamster was Papa Hamster. They all lived together in a cage in Mrs. Johnson's classroom. One day Mama Hamster baked some hamster food in the hamster oven and put it on the hamster table for breakfast. They all stood around to eat.

**Baby Hamster:** OWWWW! This hamster food is too hot!

**Mama Hamster:** You are right, Baby Hamster. What shall we do until it is cool?

**Papa Hamster:** Let's go for a run on the exercise wheel on the other side of the cage. When we come back the hamster food will be just right.

**Narrator:** The hamster family left their hamster breakfast cooling on the hamster table. They walked over to the exercise wheel inside their hamster cage to go for a morning run. While they were on the wheel, a little girl named Goldilocks, who was a student in Mrs. Johnson's class, was walking by the cage. She was on her way to get her pencil sharpened. She walked by the cage and smelled the hamster food.

**Goldilocks:** OOOHHH. That smells so good. I didn't have anything for breakfast at home. Maybe I'll just take a quick peek inside this cage.

**Narrator:** Goldilocks looked through the bars in the cage and into the little hamster house. She unlocked the cage and stuck her head right inside.

**Goldilocks:** Look at this big bowl of hamster food. I'll have to try it. Oh, no, this is just too hot. Maybe I'll eat this middle-sized bowl. No, it is just a little too cold. I'll try this tiny bowl. Oh, yes! This is just right!

**Narrator:** Goldilocks ate all the hamster food in Baby Hamster's bowl. Then she began to look around the inside of the little hamster house. She noticed the three hollow tubes that the hamsters played in.

**Goldilocks:** Look at those tubes. I think I'll stick my finger in the big one first. Goodness! This one's too big. Maybe the middle-size tube is better. No, it's still too big. I think this little one will be just right.

**Narrator:** But when Goldilocks put her big fat finger inside the tiny little tube she got stuck. She shook and shook and shook her finger until the tube flew off and smashed into a hundred pieces on the floor. That made her very angry. She decided to look around the house some more. She found the three smelly old rags that the hamsters used for their beds.

**Goldilocks:** Those smelly old rags sure do look interesting. I think I'll pick them up. I'll try the big one first. Oh, no, this is much too dirty for me. Perhaps the middle-sized one is better. No, this one's much too stinky. I'll try the little one. Yes, this one's not too dirty and not too smelly. I'll use it to blow my nose.

**Narrator:** But when Goldilocks tried to pull her head out of the cage it became stuck. Soon, the three hamsters came back from their exercise wheel.

**Baby Hamster:** Look, Father! Somebody has been in our house.

**Mama Hamster:** Let's go in very carefully and very slowly.

**Papa Hamster:** SOMEONE HAS BEEN EATING MY HAMSTER FOOD!

**Mama Hamster** SOMEONE HAS BEEN EATING MY HAMSTER FOOD!

**Baby Hamster:** SOMEONE HAS BEEN EATING MY HAMSTER FOOD! And it's all gone!

**Narrator:** The hamsters began looking around the house. Papa Hamster saw that his hollow tube had been moved.

**Papa Hamster:** SOMEONE HAS BEEN PLAYING WITH MY HOLLOW TUBE!

**Mama Hamster:** SOMEONE HAS BEEN PLAYING WITH MY HOLLOW TUBE!

**Baby Hamster:** SOMEONE HAS BEEN PLAYING WITH MY HOLLOW TUBE! And they broke it into a thousand pieces.

**Narrator:** The hamsters went to the sleeping area of their house. Papa Hamster was the first to see that his rag had been disturbed.

**Papa Hamster:** SOMEONE HAS BEEN MESSING WITH MY RAG!

**Mama Hamster:** SOMEONE HAS BEEN MESSING WITH MY RAG!

**Baby Hamster:** SOMEONE HAS BEEN MESSING WITH MY RAG! And, look, there she is with her head caught in our cage.

**Narrator:** (*faster and faster*) Goldilocks got very scared. The three hamsters began running towards her. Goldilocks pulled harder and harder. The hamsters were getting closer and closer. Goldilocks was getting more and more scared. Finally, with one last yank she pulled her head out just in the nick of time. (*slowly*) After that, she promised she would never ever eat hamster food again. The three hamsters got a large rat to guard their house and put locks on all their doors. And they all lived happily ever after.

Reprinted from Anthony D. Fredericks, *Tadpole Tales and Other Totally Terrific Treats for Readers Theatre* (Englewood, CO: Teacher Ideas Press, 1997).

# *Dear Mr. Henshaw*

## Beverly Cleary
### (New York: Morrow, 1983)

## *Summary*

Leigh Botts writes to his favorite book author. His letters are filled with questions and advice as well as a lot of revealing information about Leigh's life, his thoughts, and his feelings about his mother and father. This is a touching tale, told strictly through the correspondence of one boy; it presents a realistic and humorous look at the struggles of growing up.

## *Social Studies Disciplines*

sociology, economics, geography

## *NCSS Thematic Strands*

culture; individual development and identity; individuals, groups and institutions

## *Critical Thinking Questions*

1.  Why do you think Leigh wrote so many letters to a book author?

2.  Why would he want to tell things about his family to a person he had never met?

3.  Which author would you like to correspond with? Why?

4.  How is Leigh's life similar or different from your life? Is Leigh someone you would like to know?

5.  What would you like to ask Beverly Cleary (the author of this book)?

## *Related Books*

Bolick, Nancy. *How to Survive Your Parents' Divorce.* New York: Watts, 1995.

Brown, Marc. *Dinosaurs Divorce.* Boston: Little, Brown, 1988.

Hamilton, Kersten. *The Butterfly Book: A Kid's Guide to Attracting, Raising, and Keeping Butterflies.* Santa Fe, NM: John Muir Publications, 1997.

Hausherr, Rosmarie. *Celebrating Families.* New York: Scholastic, 1997.

Kehoe, Michael. *A Book Takes Root: The Making of a Picture Book.* New York: First Avenue, 1997.

Pringle, Laurence. *An Extraordinary Life: The Story of a Monarch Butterfly.* New York: Orchard, 1997.

Simon, Norma. *All Kinds of Families*. Champaign, IL: Albert Whitman, 1987.

Stevens, Carla. *A Book of Your Own: Keeping a Diary or Journal*. New York: Clarion, 1993.

## *Activities*

1.  Students will certainly enjoy reading other books by Beverly Cleary. Although there are many, here are a few to get them started: *Henry and Beezus* (New York: Morrow, 1952); *Mitch and Amy* (New York: Morrow, 1967); *Ramona the Pest* (New York: Morrow, 1968); and *Ramona Quimby, Age 8* (New York: Morrow, 1981).

2.  Students may enjoy creating their own electronic gadgets much as Leigh did. Various kits are available at your local Radio Shack. For students interested in constructing their own burglar alarms, Natural Science Industries produces the Electro-Tech Kit (available through science catalogs), which allows children to create a variety of electrical objects. A fascinating book for kids is *The X-Ray Picture Book of Everyday Things and How They Work* by Peter Turvey (New York: Watts, 1995).

3.  Invite students to contact local trucking firms and ask how many miles (or hours) their drivers are allowed to cover in 24 hours. With that data, invite students to name all the cities that can be reached from their town if a driver were to stay within the designated parameters. Which towns could Leigh's father drive to (from Pacific Grove, California) within the time and distance restrictions?

4.  Encourage students to read about the life and writings of Beverly Cleary. Your school or local librarian can supply several references. One particularly useful source is the author's own story: *A Girl from Yamhill* (New York: Morrow, 1988).

5.  Students may be interested in creating a large mural on the history of transportation in this country. Several teams could each research a different aspect of transportation (land, air, sea travel). Information, pictures, brochures, photos and the like can all be posted on the mural, which can then be displayed in the school library.

6.  Invite a social worker or psychologist to your classroom to talk about divorce (but *please* be sensitive to the experiences of your students). The visitor can explain some of the statistics about divorce in this country and discuss the implications for family members. How to deal with divorce and its ramifications can also become part of the presentation. Encourage students to ask questions.

7.  Students will certainly be interested in watching the development and growth of butterflies. Nasco (901 Janesville Ave., Fort Atkinson, WI 53538 [800-558-9595]) produces the Butterfly Garden, which can be ordered through their catalog or can be found in many toy and hobby stores. Students can observe and record the growth of butterflies from cocoons to adults.

8.  Invite students to create a guidebook entitled *How to Become a Better Writer*. Invite them to interview adults, teachers, business people, reporters, and other children in the community on the tips and strategies that help people write. The information they collect can be assembled into a booklet to be distributed to other classes.

9. Invite students to create an oversize collage depicting trucks and the trucking industry. Using pictures from old magazines as well as information and brochures collected from local trucking firms, students can assemble an informative collage for posting in the classroom or on a wall elsewhere in the school.

10. Invite students to compute the number of miles from Leigh's home in Pacific Grove, California to some of the other cities mentioned in the book (e.g., Bakersfield, California; Taft, California; Albuquerque, New Mexico; and Hermiston, Oregon). Later, invite students to figure out the number of miles between each of those cities and their school. These figures can be posted on a large classroom map of the United States.

11. Students may be interested in obtaining travel and tourist information about California. They can write to Office of Tourism, Box 189, Sacramento, CA 95812-0189. When material arrives, have them arrange it into an attractive display.

12. Students may enjoy setting up a pen pal network with students in another school. Contact colleagues in other schools or contact the education department of a local college and ask for the names of former students who have secured teaching positions in other parts of the state. Contact these teachers and invite their classes to correspond with the students in your class and *vice versa*. Encourage students to keep the letters flowing throughout the year (and beyond!).

13. Invite students to check the audio sections of their local library or college library for recordings or songs dealing with trucks or truck drivers (country and western songs might be a logical place to begin). Invite students to put together a listing or series of recordings of trucking songs to share with classmates. What distinguishes these songs?

14. Invite students to write a letter to Beverly Cleary commenting on this book or any other(s) she has written. Students may wish to include questions about the writing of children's books or about writing in general. Send the letter in care of Ms Cleary's publisher (William Morrow and Co., 105 Madison Ave., New York, NY 10016). Advise students that, because she receives so much mail, they may not receive a personal reply, but there's certainly no harm in trying. (By the way, Beverly Cleary's birthday is April 12—students may wish to send her a birthday card.)

15. Your students may wish to learn about children's book authors and how they write their books. Invite students to log on to the Web site of the author of this resource book (who has also written several children's books) to learn about the process of writing (**http://www.afrederickscom/author/index.html**).

# *Fire on the Mountain*

## Jane Kurtz

(New York: Simon & Schuster, 1994)

## Summary

In Ethiopia, a shepherd boy named Alemayu is challenged by a rich man to spend a night alone in the bitterly cold air of the mountains. When the master claims a false victory, Alemayu and his sister outfox the man at his own game. This is a moving and memorable tale of courage and devotion.

## Social Studies Disciplines

geography, economics, anthropology, sociology

## NCSS Thematic Strands

culture; individual development and identity; power, authority and governance

## Critical Thinking Questions

1. How did you feel about the rich man?

2. How is Alemayu similar to you or to one of your friends?

3. What would you have done to fool or trick the rich man?

4. Would you want to live the life of a shepherd? Why or why not?

5. What did you enjoy most about this story?

## Related Books

Aardema, Verna. *Bringing the Rain to Kapiti Plain*. New York: Dial Press, 1981.

Araujo, Frank. *The Perfect Orange: A Tale from Ethiopia*. New York: Rayve Productions, 1994.

Courlander, Harold. *The Fire on the Mountain and Other Stories from Ethiopia and Eritrea*. New York: Henry Holt, 1995.

Fradin, Dennis. *Ethiopia*. Chicago: Children's Press, 1994.

Gray, Nigel. *A Country Far Away*. New York: Orchard, 1989.

Jenkins, Earnestine. *Glorious Past: Ancient Egypt, Ethiopia, and Namibia*. New York: Chelsea House, 1994.

## *Activities*

1.  Invite your students to collect current and pertinent information about Ethiopia from **http://www.africanet.com/africanet/country/ethiopia/home.htm**. Students may wish to assemble their information into an illustrative booklet for placement in the school library.

2.  Students can access the Ethiopian embassy through the following Web site: **http://www.nicom.com/~ethiopia/index.htm**. They may wish to contact the embassy for additional information and share that data with other students in the school.

3.  Your students may enjoy a typical food from Africa. Following is a recipe for *kanya*, a popular sweetmeat in many African countries.

### KANYA

Thoroughly mix $\frac{1}{2}$ cup smooth peanut butter and $\frac{1}{2}$ cup superfine sugar in a large bowl. Press the granules of sugar against the side of the bowl with a wooden spoon until they are completely crushed and mixed with the peanut butter.

Slowly add $\frac{2}{3}$ cup of uncooked Cream of Rice and continue stirring until the mixture is completely and thoroughly blended.

Spread the mixture in a loaf pan and press down with your hands until it is evenly spread. Cover the pan with plastic wrap and refrigerate for two to three hours until firm.

Cut into small bars and enjoy!

4.  Students may wish to make their own version of oxtail soup (another popular food in several African countries). Here's a recipe:

### OXTAIL SOUP

Boil oxtails in a large pot until the meat falls off the bones. This may require simmering for several hours (if oxtails are not available at a local butcher shop, use beef bones).

Have students bring in vegetables of their choice. Put the vegetables in the pot along with the oxtails and three to four quarts of water. Season to taste and simmer for another hour.

Have a student recorder keep a list of the ingredients used in the soup and develop it into an original recipe. Send the recipe home or invite parents to come in and enjoy the soup with your class.

*Note:* Other ingredients such as beans, rice, or macaroni can also be added to the soup.

5.  Invite students make a time line showing the sequence of events leading up to the feast (This can be written and illustrated on a large roll of butcher paper and hung across one or two walls of the classroom). Talk about the planning that leads up to an event of this type. Next, have students plan for a classroom feast or similar event. Have them make up a comparable time line to be hung in proximity to Alemayu's time line. Discuss any differences.

6.  Invite students make mosaics of cows. Instruct them to use various kinds of seeds, beans, split peas, rice, macaroni, and spices to create their mosaics. These can be painted with watercolors and hung throughout the room.

7.  Invite students to imagine they were invited to the rich man's feast. Encourage them to research the forms of transportation they could use to get to Ethiopia, how much it would cost, and how long it would take them to get there. Invite them to locate Ethiopia on a map and trace the route they would follow for each form of transportation they consider. Invite a local travel agent to class to discuss the advantages of different forms of transportation regarding pleasure, cost, efficiency, etc.

8.  Students may enjoy creating a tabletop model of an Ethiopian village. Cardboard cutouts of animals can be combined with pipe-cleaner people and toothpick houses to create the village. Blue cellophane can be crinkled and used to represent a river. Invite students to label the various parts of their village.

9.  Students may enjoy writing a letter to a U.S. Embassy in one or more African countries. The addresses of specific embassies can be obtained from the Department of State (2201 C St. NW, Washington, DC 20520). Students should decide on the type of information they would like to receive from a specific embassy (brochures, agriculture facts, type of government, etc.) before drafting their letters. As information is received, it can be posted on a collective bulletin board and reviewed throughout the year.

10. Divide the class into two groups. Assign one group the task of writing a prequel to the story; the other group the task of writing a sequel. Encourage students to discuss the various types of events and actions they could include in their additions.

11. Invite students to study several maps of Africa and then create (using colored tape) an outline of the continent on the classroom floor. Encourage students to stand around the edges of the outline, holding hands if necessary, to "become" the shape of Africa. Have students sit down in place and sing "Kumbaya"—a traditional African folk song (*Book of Kidsongs* by Nancy and John Cassidy [Palo Alto, CA: Klutz Press, 1986]).

12. Invite students to create puppets of the story characters by decorating old socks with markers, colored paper, bits of yarn, or other scraps. Divide the class into small groups and assign one scene from the story to each group. Encourage each group to paint a background on butcher paper or an old bed sheet. Hang the background on a bulletin board or use a table turned on its side for the puppet theater.

13. Provide students with old white bed sheets and fabric scraps. Have students create costumes similar to those worn by the characters in the story (use the book as a guide). Students can then dramatize their favorite parts of the story.

14. Have an African foods celebration. Bring in a variety of foods native to Africa: honey, dates, coffee, cloves (try clove gum), yams, sunflower seeds, peanuts, grapes, and olives. Invite students each to write a paragraph describing their reactions to the foods and encourage them to choose their favorite African food.

15. Invite students to write a sequel to the story titled *How the Rich Man Learned Kindness.*

# On the Day You Were Born
## Debra Frasier
(New York: Harcourt Brace Jovanovich, 1991)

## Summary

A touching and moving account of the natural events that occur on the day of one's birth. The movement of animals, the turn of the planets, and the production of oxygen are all detailed in this brilliantly executed book that is a "must have" for any classroom or living room.

## Social Studies Disciplines

sociology, anthropology, geography

## NCSS Thematic Strands

time, continuity, and change; people, places, and environment; individual development and identity; individuals, groups, and institutions; global connections

## Critical Thinking Questions

1. How did this book relate to the day you were born?

2. What would you like to say to the author of this book?

3. What was so special about the day you were born?

4. What makes you special?

5. Which page in the book was most beautiful?

6. How did your family celebrate the day of your birth?

## Related Books

Archambault, John. *The Birth of a Whale*. New York: Silver Burdett, 1996.
Carlson, Nancy. *I Like Me*. New York: Viking, 1988.
Knight, Margy. *Welcoming Babies*. New York: Tilbury House, 1994.
Spirn, Michael. *Birth*. New York: Blackbirch, 1998.
Watanabe, Shigeo. *It's My Birthday*. New York: G. P. Putnam's Sons, 1988.

## *Activities*

1. Invite each student to interview his or her parents and other relatives about their recollections of the child's birth. Students may be interested in obtaining more than one retelling of their births to determine whether different people remember the births the same way. When completed, students may wish to gather their data together into an indexed directory of important events surrounding their births.

2. Encourage students to record important events from their own lives—one event on each of several index cards. Hang some strings along one wall of your classroom or overhead. Provide students with several clothespins and ask each one to select a string and hang his or her cards along the string in sequence. Provide opportunities for each student to describe his or her time line.

3. Invite students to visit **http://www.kidsparties.com/traditions.htm**. Here they can discover various traditions around the world for celebrating birthdays. Students can gather information on how birthday parties got started, on birthday celebrations in various countries, on famous people's birthdays, and on special family traditions. Invite students to add their own family-related information to that obtained from this site.

4. Invite students to visit **http://www.yahooligans.com/docs/tdih/**. Here they can discover who was born on any day in recorded history—including their own birthdays.

5. For each student, tape a sheet of newsprint on one wall of the classroom. Place a child between the paper and the light from an overhead projector so that a silhouette of the child's head is projected on the newsprint. Invite another student to trace the silhouette on the paper. Do this for each student in the class. Encourage students to cut out their silhouettes and record important events from their early lives on the paper. Each silhouette can be highlighted with a watercolor wash and hung in an appropriate place in the classroom. As additional events occur during the year, students should be encouraged to add them to their silhouettes.

6. Invite each student to create a personal newspaper. For example, under the heading *Sports,* children can write about the physical activities they participate in regularly. Under *Horoscopes,* they can record personal predictions; under *Fashion,* the clothes they like to wear; and under *Music,* their favorite songs. Encourage children to decide which headlines or categories they would like to include in their personal newspapers. Make sure these are "published" and shared with all students.

7. Students may wish to create personal time lines using photographs brought from home. Encourage students to bring in several photos of themselves; they can then post the photos in sequence on an appropriate bulletin board. Students can also write a short caption for each picture describing what the picture portrays, the approximate date, and what it means to the individual child.

8. Invite each student to ask friends, family, and acquaintances for a list of single adjectives that best describe his or her birth or first few days after birth. When students have collected an adequate sampling of adjectives, invite them to sort the adjectives into several categories (e.g., adjectives related to size, adjectives related to personality,

adjectives related to temperament). Other categories could include *adjectives from family*, *adjectives from friends*, and *adjectives from myself*. Allow students to decide which categories they want to use. Each student's list can be collected in a large class scrapbook decorated with photos of all the children.

9. Invite students to create family alphabet books. Provide each student with 26 sheets of paper. Encourage students to write one letter of the alphabet on each sheet of paper. For each letter, invite each student to choose a word or phrase that describes something about his or her early life. When the project is completed, students may wish to bind their sheets between two sheets of cardboard to create personal alphabet books.

10. Invite each child to lie on a sheet of butcher paper or newsprint. Encourage another child to trace an outline of the child on the paper. Invite each child to cut out his or her outline and post it on a wall of the classroom. During the next several weeks, have the children record positive phrases or observations in each classmates' outline. Keep these up throughout the year and encourage children to continue adding comments in the outlines of their classmates. You should also put up an outline of yourself in which students can record appropriate observations (positive, of course).

11. Encourage students to write a sequel to this book. The sequels could be titled *On the Day You Turned One, On the Day You Were Five, On the Day You Learned to Read* or a similar personal topic. Plan time for students to share their essays.

12. Invite each child to imagine that he or she is a newborn baby in a hospital nursery. What would they like to say to the other infants in the nursery? What kinds of things or people do they see? What kinds of experiences do they have?

13. Share several newspaper ads with your students. Then, ask each student to create an original ad about himself or herself (as though they were items for sale). Which of their qualities would they want to emphasize in a limited amount of space? What special features do they have that others would enjoy? Students may wish to emphasize physical or personality characteristics, or both. Post these in a prominent location in the room.

14. Invite students to "produce" some sort of celebration that heralds their births. What will the animals do? What will happen in nature? How will various parts of the Earth react?

15. Invite each student to select one of the animals mentioned in the book. Encourage students to investigate the circumstances surrounding the birth of one of those animals. What makes that birth so special? How is the birth of that offspring similar to or different from the birth of other animals? Students may wish to contact the high school biology teacher or a professor from the biology department at a local college. When students have gathered their information they may wish to assemble it into a portfolio or binder.

16. Invite students to create an original and special birth announcement for themselves. Share "regular" birth announcements and then invite students to design their own that herald and joyfully announce their arrivals into the world. What, specifically, would they like to have celebrated?

# Tapenum's Day: A Wampanoag Indian Boy in Pilgrim Times
## Kate Waters
(New York: Scholastic, 1996)

## Summary

This book explores the life of a Wampanoag Indian boy in the 1620s. It is an intimate and accurate portrayal of native life in America during European colonization. The focus is on Tapenum, who has not been chosen as a warrior counselor, and his plan to strengthen his physical and spiritual skills so that he might be chosen in the future. This book offers wonderful insights into both the human spirit and colonial life. It is also part of a three-book series (*Sarah Morton's Day* and *Samuel Eaton's Day*) by the same author.

## Social Studies Disciplines

anthropology, sociology, history, economics

## NCSS Thematic Strands

culture; time, continuity, and change; people, places, and environment; individual development and identity; production, distribution, and consumption; civic ideals and practices

## Critical Thinking Questions

1.  How is Tapenum similar to you or to one of your friends?

2.  How is life for Tapenum and his family different from your life?

3.  Why was it so important for Tapenum to become a *pniese*?

4.  What else could Tapenum have done to prepare himself to become a warrior counselor?

5.  Would you enjoy having Tapenum as one of your friends?

6.  Would you like to trade places with Tapenum, even for one day?

7.  What are some of the tasks you do during the day that are similar to those done by Tapenum?

## Related Books

McGovern, Ann. *If You Sailed on the Mayflower in 1620*. New York: Scholastic, 1993.

Penner, Lucille. *Eating the Plates: A Pilgrim Book of Food and Manners*. New York: Simon & Schuster, 1991.

Roop, Connie. *Pilgrim Voices: Our First Year in the New World*. New York: Walker, 1998.

San Souci, Robert. *N. C. Wyeth's Pilgrims*. San Francisco, CA: Chronicle Books, 1996.

Sewall, Marcia. *The Pilgrims of Plimoth*. New York: Aladdin, 1996.

Stamper, Judith. *New Friends in a New Land: A Thanksgiving Story*. Austin, TX: Steck-Vaughn, 1992.

Waters, Kate. *On the Mayflower: Voyage of the Ship's Apprentice & a Passenger Girl*. New York: Scholastic, 1996.

———. *Samuel Eaton's Day*. New York: Scholastic, 1996.

———. *Sarah Morton's Day*. New York: Scholastic, 1989.

## Activities

1. Invite students to create a bulletin board display of the Wampanoag words used in the book (a glossary is provided in the back of the book). Encourage students to accompany each definition with an original illustration.

2. Encourage students to maintain a daily journal of their activities, tasks, and chores. If possible, invite selected students to have someone take photographs of some of those activities. The descriptions and photos can be mounted together in a descriptive notebook titled *(student's name) Day*.

3. Set up a special bulletin board titled *My Goals*. Encourage each child to post one or more goals he or she has for the coming week. Take time to discuss the importance of goal setting and ways that students need to attend to their self-initiated goals. At the end of each week take time (as a class) to discuss those goals, whether they were reached, and what might be done in the future to help them achieve their goals. Invite students to compare their goals with those established by Tapenum.

4. If possible, invite students to grow corn either in the classroom or in a selected location on the school grounds. If the corn is to be grown indoors, plan to set up a deep wooden box filled with soil and a grow light. Invite students to read the directions on a packet of corn and to plant and tend the seeds according to those instructions. What challenges do they meet in growing their own corn? How is growing corn (either outdoors or indoors) different from the way Tapenum's family grew corn more than 350 years ago?

5. Invite your students to construct models, using a variety of art materials, of the buildings and dwellings depicted in the book. Encourage students to construct a model village for display in the classroom or school library.

6. Invite each student to write or illustrate an event in her or his life about which they are especially proud. Establish a display area or bulletin board for students to post these affirmations. Students may also elect to create a classroom notebook (with the title *I am proud of...*) to which every student can add selections that complete the sentence stem. Students can create and discuss these statements regularly.

7. When hunting, the Wampanoag Indians frequently carried dried corn for their meals (as did Tapenum in the story). Invite students to create their own version of dried corn using the following recipe:

### DRIED CORN

✓ three ears of sweet corn

Cut all the kernels from the ears of corn (this should be done by an adult). Spread the kernels one layer deep on a cookie sheet. Bake in a slow oven (175 degrees) for several hours until the kernels are dry. Allow to cool. Serve small portions to each student (be aware of any food allergies).

8. The early colonists also relied on corn as a staple. Johnnycakes were popular with those who traveled far from home; here's the recipe:

**JOHNNYCAKES**

✓ 1 egg

✓ 2 cups of cornmeal

✓ ¾ teaspoon of salt

✓ 1½ cups of milk

✓ butter

Beat the egg in a medium-sized mixing bowl. Stir in the cornmeal, salt, and milk and mix thoroughly. Drop spoonfuls of the batter in a well-greased frying pan. Fry until brown on both sides. Serve hot with butter.

(*Note*: Students may wish to experiment with Johnnycakes as a traveling meal. Invite them to prepare several Johnnycakes and store them in a covered container for several days. Invite students to bring in their Johnnycakes for lunch. Plan time after lunch to discuss whether they would enjoy eating the Johnnycakes regularly.)

9. Invite students to work in groups to create a travel brochure for the New World. What should be emphasized? Which features of the New World should be depicted in the brochure? What should not be included in the brochure? Photographs would be a valuable part of these brochures.

10. Because the Wampanoag Indians did not have refrigeration, foods had to be preserved in other ways. Invite students to investigate the different ways of preserving food. They may wish to bring in several types of fruits and allow them to dry in the sun for a few days to create fruit jerky. (First, cut the fruit into thin strips. Next, lay the strips on pieces of cardboard and cover with cheesecloth. Be sure to bring the fruit in each evening and put it out each morning until it is dried.) Invite students to experiment with different types of fruit to see which one dries best and tastes best.

11. Invite students to calculate the distance from Namasket (the Wampanoag Indian village) to the following locations:
    a. their home towns
    b. Washington, D.C.
    c. London, England
    a. a non-North American site where their relatives grew up

   Encourage students to plot those distances on a map of the world. Display the map on a bulletin board and use string to represent the various distances and locations.

12. Students may wish to create their own version of *Jeopardy*. Invite one group of students to create various answers from the book and present them to a second group. The second group could create the corresponding questions for those answers.

13. Provide each student with a long rectangular piece of black or brown felt (e.g., 2-x-14 inches). Place a squash seed at the end of each piece of felt, fold it over, and wet it down. Add a new squash seed every two or three days, fold over the felt, and wet it down. Keep these felt seed packets in a dark place. After a week or so, invite students to check the growth of their seeds. Later, some of the seeds may be transplanted to a growing area on the school grounds.

14. Obtain a large sheet of newsprint. Invite individual students to stand between the sheet and an overhead projector. Turn on the projector and ask each student to assume one of the poses Tapenum took in the story. Encourage other students to trace the outline of each silhouette on the newsprint. Create several silhouettes and invite students to color them and post them around the room.

15. Some students may wish to play charades. They can illustrate one or more of Tapenum's actions for other students to guess.

16. If possible, borrow some costumes from your local high school or college drama department. Invite students to create an original skit about a day in the life of a Wampanoag Indian girl. Which activities or chores would the girl do that would be similar to or different from those of Tapenum?

17. Students may wish to initiate secret pen pal journals with other students in the school or at another school. Without revealing the names of their pen pals, invite students to write to an individual and share parts of his or her day. You can act as the messenger (or mail person) and deliver those messages from one school or classroom to yours.

18. Invite students to write to the address below to obtain information and/or brochures about Plimouth Plantation:

    Plimouth Plantation
    P.O. Box 1620
    Plymouth, MA 02360

    Additionally, students may wish to take a virtual tour of Plimoth Plantation. They can do so at one of the following Web sites:

    **http://www.plimoth.org**

    **http://pilgrims.net/plimothplantation/vtour/index.htm**

19. Students may enjoy making Indian corn bread in much the same way as the American Indians made it:

## CORN BREAD

Boil three cups of water and stir in one cup of cornmeal grits. Simmer until all the water is absorbed. Allow to cool and turn onto a work surface that has been floured with a cup of fine cornmeal flour. Work the mixture into two round flat cakes. Bake on a floured cookie sheet at 400 degrees for about 45 minutes.

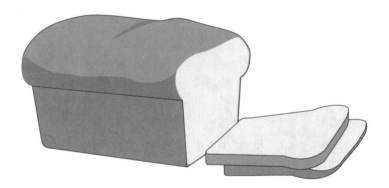

# The Whipping Boy
## Sid Fleischman
(New York: Greenwillow Books, 1986)

## Summary

Jemmy, who must be whipped every time the prince gets into trouble, leads the young Highness through the forests and sewers of Olde England in an adventure filled with suspense, strange characters, and the coming of age of "Prince Brat."

## Social Studies Disciplines

sociology, political science, economics, history

## NCSS Thematic Strands

culture; time, continuity and change; people, places and environment; individual development and identity; individuals, groups and institutions; power, authority and governance; civic ideals and practices

## Critical Thinking Questions

1.  What would you enjoy most about living during the time of Jemmy and Prince Brat. Why?

2.  Is Prince Brat similar to anyone you know? In what ways?

3.  What types of adventures do you think the two boys would get into in a sequel to this story?

4.  How would Prince Brat's inability to read have been a problem for him later in life?

5.  Describe what you would need in order to live in a sewer.

## Related Books

Brightling, Geoff. *Medieval Life*. New York: Alfred A. Knopf, 1996.

Deary, Terry. *The Measly Middle Ages*. New York: Scholastic, 1998.

Hanawalt, Barbara. *Middle Ages: An Illustrated History*. New York: Oxford University Press, 1998.

MacDonald, Fiona. *How Would You Survive in the Middle Ages?* New York: Watts, 1995.

Raintree Editorial Staff. *The Early Middle Ages*. Austin, TX: Steck-Vaughn, 1990.

Reid, Stuart. *Castles Under Siege*. Austin, TX: Steck-Vaughn, 1998.

## *Activities*

1. Invite students to suggest some ideas or strategies that would help the young prince learn to read. What do students do during their reading lessons that would be helpful to the prince?

2. Invite several students to investigate the life cycle of one of the animals mentioned in the story (e.g., horse, bear, cow, rat). Students can assemble this information into a poster or an oral report to share with the class.

3. Students may wish to create a line of greeting cards that could have been used by characters in the story. For example, what type of card would Billy and Cutwater send the king? What type of card would the prince want to send his father at the end of the story?

4. Some students may wish to create an imaginary journal that could have been written by the prince (if he could write). Entries could include the various adventures the two youngsters got into, the characters they saw along the way, and how they eventually settled their differences.

5. Invite students to create imaginary advertisements for some of the characters at the fair and to imagine that each character is going to put an ad in the local newspaper. What information should be included in the ads to attract more business?

6. Bring in a large bag of potatoes and have students practice addition or multiplication using potatoes in various arrangements and sets.

7. Demonstrate how various instruments can imitate the motions or movements of animals. For example, a flute can be played to depict a bird, a tuba can depict a bear. You may find it helpful to play recordings of *Peter and the Wolf* and *Carnival of the Animals* so that students can hear how different instruments approximate various animals.

8. Encourage several students to write a sequel to the story. What kinds of new adventures would the two young boys get into now? Would their friendship blossom or would they fall into their old familiar ways?

9. Invite students to locate various dimensions of the animals mentioned in the story. For example, what is the average weight of a rat, how long is it, how tall? This information can be graphed on a sheet of oaktag.

10. Some students may wish to investigate the differences between the English and American monetary systems. What are their differences or similarities?

11. Encourage students to create an animal collage by cutting out various pictures of cows, rats, horses, and bears from nature or environmental magazines. They can post the pictures on construction paper and display them throughout the room.

12. Invite students to check the local yellow pages for modern-day services that might be used by royalty. Examples may include carpet cleaning services (for the red carpet), butlers, cooks, transportation services, etc.

13. Ask students to interview their parents, grandparents, or relatives about family stories, folk tales, or legends they learned as children. If some families have recently immigrated to this country, you may want to invite children's relatives to class to share stories and legends from their countries of origin.

14. Encourage students to investigate the different types of costumes people wore during the time of this story. What kinds of clothes did rich people wear? What kinds of clothes did poor people wear? What were the differences?

15. Ask students to locate current prices for some of the items mentioned in the story. For example, how much does a bar of soap cost? A bag of potatoes? A horse? A clove of garlic? To what can they attribute the variations in prices?

16. Invite students to create or put together various homemade instruments that could be used in retelling the story. For example, the sound of two coconut shells pounded on a hard surface can imitate a horse's trot or gallop. Two sandpaper blocks rubbed together can imitate the sound of the boys walking slowly through the fog-shrouded forest. Rubbing wet fingers around the rim of a glass can imitate the sound of the sewer rats.

17. Invite your students to discover interesting facts and delightful information about the castles of England, Wales, and Scotland by logging on to **http://www.personal. psu.edu/faculty/n/x/nxd10/castles.htm#top**.

18. Encourage students to pretend they are news reporters covering the kidnapping of the prince. Which facts or details would they include in a television broadcast? Which ones would be appropriate for a newspaper article?

19. Direct students to construct an imaginary map of the prince's kingdom. Be sure to have them include all the sites mentioned in the story as well as any others they think would be important in a kingdom.

20. Students may enjoy listening to *The Lady and the Unicorn* (recording by John Renbourn, Warner Bros.)—a collection of medieval music, folk tunes, and early classical music on guitars, sitar, hand-drums, glockenspiel, viola, concertina, flutes, and violin.

21. Ask students to collect several copies of travel magazines and prepare one description of England as it was in the time of this story and another description of England as it exists today. How do these two descriptions differ?

22. Invite students to research the history of fairs and carnivals. How have they changed over the years? Which events at today's fairs are identical to the fairs of long ago?

23. Students may wish to log on to **http://www.tqjunior.advanced.org/4051/** to take a journey through the Middle Ages—a journey developed by students at Salford Hills Elementary School.

24. Give students small slices of garlic, onion, potato, and apple and ask them to taste each one. What differences or similarities do they notice? Afterwards, blindfold several students and ask them to hold their noses. Give each student slices of the same foods as before, but randomly. Ask each student to explain why he or she had difficulty distinguishing them.

25. Some students may enjoy looking into the nutritional needs of various people and animals mentioned in the story. They can turn this information into a chart that lists the daily nutritional needs of growing children, adults, bears, rats, cows, and horses. What are the similarities and/or differences between these individuals?

26. Invite students to investigate differences in sanitation during the time of this story and today. How do we dispose of our wastes in comparison with how wastes were disposed of years ago? Why is sanitation such an important urban and/or environmental issue?

# Chapter 5

## Family

## Animal Dads
### Sneed Collard
(Boston: Houghton Mifflin, 1997)

## Summary

In this whimsical and intriguing exploration of fatherhood in the animal kingdom, we observe a wide range of surprising parenting skills. There are helpful dads, playful dads, hunting dads, baby-sitting dads, and even dads that give birth. This book is a delightful accompaniment to any family unit.

## Social Studies Disciplines

sociology, anthropology

## NCSS Thematic Strands

culture; individual development and identity; individuals, groups, and institutions

## Critical Thinking Questions

1.  Which animal father did you find the most amazing?

2.  Was there an animal dad in this book who was similar to any human father you know?

3.  How are animal fathers similar to human fathers?

4.  What is amazing about your own father?

5.  How did the illustrations help you enjoy this book?

## Related Books

Adler, C. S. *Daddy's Climbing Tree*. New York: Clarion, 1993.

Alden, Laura. *Father's Day*. New York: Children's Press, 1995.

Burke, Maggie. *When Daddy Comes to Visit*. New York: Winston-Derek, 1997.

Merriam, Eve. *Daddies at Work*. New York: Aladdin, 1996.

Morris, Ann. *The Daddy Book*. New York: Silver Press, 1995.

Rotner, Shelley. *Lots of Dads*. New York: Dial Books for Young Readers, 1997.

## Activities

1.  All the illustrations in this book were created with torn paper. Invite your students to analyze the illustrations and then to experiment in creating their own torn-paper illustrations. Students may wish to illustrate a family scene or an activity they participate in with their fathers. Be sure these are prominently displayed in the classroom.

2.  Invite students to select one each of the animals portrayed in this book. Encourage each child to assume the role or persona of that animal and then to write an imaginary diary entry (or series of entries) about *A Day with My Father*. Each student may elect to choose play-time activities, caring activities, feeding activities, or any other combination of activities to describe the relationship between the offspring and its father.

3.  Invite each youngster to write a letter of appreciation to his or her own father. What would they like to acknowledge or celebrate about their fathers? What makes their fathers so special? What role have their fathers played in their upbringing that they would like to mention?

4.  Encourage students to create Father's Day greeting cards that could be sent on a special day of the year (not necessarily on the third Sunday in June). Students may wish to designate a day in the fall or spring as Father's Day and celebrate the accomplishments of their respective fathers.

5.  Invite students to create a skit or play that depicts one or more paternal events described in the book. For example, students could create a skit that highlights the different ways that animal and human fathers play with their offspring. Or students may wish to put together a production that illustrates the various ways fathers obtain food for their families.

6.  Invite students to log on to **http://www.holidays.net/fathers**. This is a wonderful and all-inclusive site (check out the background music) that commemorates and celebrates fathers and father figures (stepfathers, uncles, grandfathers) around the world; it provides stories to read, puzzles and games to play, and various ways to honor every father. A great site!

7.  At **http://www.agirlsworld.com/amy/pajama/fathersday/index.html**, the girls in your classroom can list and read about *The Coolest Thing My Dad Ever Did, The Funniest Thing My Dad Ever Did,* and *The Bravest Thing My Dad Ever Did.*

8.  Invite students to create posters on the importance of fathers reading with their children. If possible, obtain permission from several local businesses to display the posters in store windows or near cash registers. Every so often, your students may wish to create new posters and rotate them.

9.  Invite students to create a family newspaper. Each child is a reporter for his or her family and contributes articles about some of the jobs, tasks, duties, and responsibilities accomplished by his or her father. Gather the articles and "publish" them as *The Father Times.*

10. Provide students with modeling clay and invite each one to create a bust of an important male in their lives (e.g., father, uncle, grandfather, special friend). Plan time for each student to share the reasons his or her selected individual was or is significant. When the busts are completed, set up a special gallery in the classroom.

11. Contact a local community center or senior citizens home and establish an adopt-a-grandfather program. Each student can be assigned one of the residents as his or her "foster grandfather." Students may wish to correspond or pen pal (via regular mail or e-mail) with their surrogate grandfathers over an extended period.

12. Invite students to interview people in their households, neighborhoods, or communities on what it takes to be a good father. Encourage students to meet in small groups, share the collected information, and then create an informative brochure; they can distribute the brochure through a local community agency.

13. Invite each student to bring in a special memento or article that represents his or her own father. This may be a piece of clothing, a newspaper article, a photograph, a trophy. Invite youngsters to share the value and significance of these items with the class.

14. If possible, contact a local men's group and invite several members into your classroom for a panel discussion. Encourage students to question the visitors on what it takes to be a father. What are the duties and responsibilities of fatherhood? How do fathers provide for the family? What makes being a father so special?

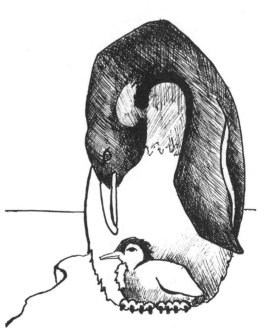

# Fly Away Home
## Eve Bunting
### (New York: Clarion, 1991)

## Summary

This is a touching story about a young boy and his father who are homeless and live in an airport. The book tells how they elude security people, obtain food, and learn to survive by their wits. A poignant story, it is filled with hope and determination for a better life. A wonderful read-aloud story for every classroom.

## Social Studies Disciplines

sociology, economics

## NCSS Thematic Strands

culture; individual development and identity; individuals, groups and institutions; production, distribution, and consumption; civic ideals and practices

## Critical Thinking Questions

1.  Why did the author include the little story about the bird trapped inside the airport?

2.  What events do you think happened that led to the boy and his father living in the airport?

3.  What will the boy and his father need to do to move into their own apartment?

4.  Do you think the events of this story happen on a regular basis? Please explain.

## Related Books

Arnold, Caroline. *Children of the Settlement Houses.* Minneapolis, MN: Carolrhoda, 1998.

Ayer, Eleanor. *Homeless Children.* New York: Lucent Books, 1997.

Berck, Judith. *No Place to Be: Voices of Homeless Children.* New York: Houghton Mifflin, 1992.

Johnson, Joan. *Kids Without Homes.* New York: Watts, 1991.

McCauslin, Mark. *Homelessness.* Mankato, MN: Crestwood House, 1994.

Nichelason, Margery. *Homeless or Hopeless?* Minneapolis, MN: Lerner, 1994.

Switzer, Ellen. *Anyplace But Here: Young, Alone, and Homeless: What to Do.* New York: Atheneum, 1992.

## *Activities*

1. Plan time to talk with students about homeless people in this country. What events cause people or families to become homeless? Should we treat homeless people any differently than we treat people who live in houses or apartments? How can homeless people be helped? Plan time for students to share their thoughts and perceptions.

2. If possible, visit a local homeless shelter or social service agency and ask about some of the services provided for homeless individuals and families. You may wish to invite a representative to visit your classroom and share thoughts and ideas with your students; encourage students to prepare a list of questions beforehand.

3. Invite your students to write a letter to the editor of the local newspaper about the plight of homeless people in this country. Encourage students to address homelessness as not just happening to those of low socioeconomic standing, but as affecting people from many walks of life.

4. Encourage students to write a fictitious letter to the young boy in the story. What words of support can students share with the boy that would give him hope for a better future?

5. The following Web sites will provide your students with insights about homeless people and how the issue of homelessness is being addressed in this country. (*Note:* Some of the information on these sites may be disturbing to some youngsters. I suggest that you take time to review the sites before offering them to your students.)

   **http://www.victimservices.org/travhlp.html**

   **http://earthsystems.org/ways/**

   **http://www.commnet.edu/QVCTC/student/GaryOKeefe/
   homeless/frame.html**

   **http://aspe.os.dhhs.gov/progsys/homeless/**

6. Invite students to create a sequel to the story. What happens to the boy and his father in one month? In one year? In five years? Be sure to plan time for all students to share their stories.

7. Encourage students to work in small groups to create a scrapbook of all the places they have lived during their lives. Invite students to collect photos from old magazines and assemble them into various categories (houses, apartment buildings, trailer parks, etc.).

8. Encourage students to approach the oldest living relative in each of their families and conduct an interview. The interview can be conducted in person, by telephone, or by mail. Invite students to inquire about some of the most memorable homes or living arrangements of their relatives. Provide opportunities for students to speak or write about their discoveries.

9. Students may enjoy creating a classroom newspaper on homelessness. Assign them the roles of reporters and ask them to interview family members about their opinions of homelessness and/or homeless people. Students can assemble the information from each family into a sheet of news and then collect the sheets into a large newspaper.

10. Invite students to bring in photographs of various family members. Encourage students to use pushpins on a large world map to indicate where each family member has lived; post the photographs next to those cities and states.

11. Invite students to create a collage (pictures and words cut from old magazines and glued to a sheet of poster board) of the most important things in family life (e.g., love, sharing, conversation, listening, caring, etc.). Invite students to discuss the role of shelter as a family need.

12. For each student, tape a sheet of newsprint on one wall of the classroom. Place a child between the paper and the light from an overhead projector so that a silhouette of the child's head is projected onto the newsprint. Invite another student to trace the silhouette on the paper. Do this for each student in the class. Encourage students to cut out their individual silhouettes and write about important events concerning their families on the paper. They can then highlight the silhouettes with a watercolor wash and hang them in an appropriate place in the classroom. Encourage students to add additional events to their silhouettes as those events occur during the year.

13. Invite students to create family alphabet books. Provide each student with 26 sheets of paper. Encourage students to write one letter of the alphabet on each sheet of paper. For each letter, invite students to choose a word or phrase that describes something about themselves or their families and record it on the appropriate sheet. When this task is completed, students may wish to bind their sheets between two sheets of cardboard to create a complete family alphabet book.

14. Invite each child to lie on a sheet of butcher paper or newsprint. Ask another child to trace an outline of the child on the paper. Invite each child to cut out his or her outline and post it on a wall of the classroom. During the next several weeks, invite students to write in each of their classmates' outlines; encourage them to record positive phrases or observations about the specific individual. Encourage children to add comments in the outlines of their classmates continuously throughout the school year. You may wish to put up an outline of yourself; invite students to record appropriate observations (positive, of course).

15. Share several real estate ads with your students. Then, invite students to create original ads about their homes (as though they were putting them up for sale). What would they choose to emphasize in a limited space? Which special features do they think others would enjoy? Students may wish to emphasize aesthetic features rather than physical characteristics. Post the ads prominently in the classroom.

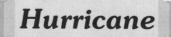

# *Hurricane*
## Jonathan London
(New York: Lothrop, Lee & Shepard, 1998)

## Summary

This is a touching and evocative story about a family in Puerto Rico and how they prepare for an oncoming hurricane. Told through the eyes of a young boy, it puts a human face on a natural disaster and its aftermath. The strength of the family is realistically portrayed and wonderfully described in this engaging tale.

## Social Studies Disciplines

geography, sociology, economics

## NCSS Thematic Strands

time, continuity, and change; people, places, and environment; individuals, groups, and institutions; production, distribution, and consumption; civic ideals and practices

## Critical Thinking Questions

1.  What was the most frightening aspect of this story?

2.  Why was it important for the family to leave the house?

3.  What might be some of the chores family members will have to do after the hurricane?

4.  Have you ever been in a scary situation with your family? How did you react?

5.  Why was everyone singing in the shelter?

## Related Books

Ancona, George. *Barrio: Jose's Neighborhood.* New York: Harcourt Brace, 1998.
Erlbach, Arlene. *Hurricanes.* New York: Children's Press, 1993.
Fradin, Dennis. *Puerto Rico.* New York: Grolier, 1998.
Hausherr, Rosemarie. *Celebrating Families.* New York: Scholastic, 1997.
Johnston, Joyce. *Puerto Rico.* Minneapolis, MN: Lerner, 1994.
Kent, Deborah. *Puerto Rico.* New York: Children's Press, 1991.
Souza, D.M. *Hurricanes.* Minneapolis, MN: Carolrhoda, 1996.
Wiesner, David. *Hurricane.* New York: Clarion, 1990.

## *Activities*

1.  Students may be interested in obtaining information and relevant facts about hurricanes. The following Web sites provide a wealth of information:

    **http://www.reedbooks.com.au/rigby/hot/hurrwh1.html**

    **http://www.macontelegraph.com/special/hurr/hurr.htm**

    **http://www.jannws.state.ms.us/hrcn.html**

    **http://www.sun-sentinal.com/storm/history/**

    **http://www.miamisci.org/hurricane/hurricane0.html**

2.  Students may be interested in seeing realtime videos of hurricanes that have hit the United States in recent years. They can do so at the following Web sites:

    **http://rsd.gsfc.nasa.gov/rsd/movies/movies.html**

    **http://www.discovery.com/stories/science/hurricanes/
    hurricanes.html**

    When students have seen one or more of these videos, invite them to imagine that they were in the path of one of those storms. Encourage students to discuss their feelings about being in such a destructive and violent natural disaster.

3. Following are several Web sites about Puerto Rico that your students may find interesting:

   **http://www.house.gov/romero-barcelo/about.htm**

   **http://www.ocdi.gov/cia/publications/factbook/rq.html**

   **http://welcome.topuertorico.org**

   **http://www.puertoricousa.com**

4. When students have had an opportunity to visit one or more of the sites above, invite them to develop appropriate travel brochures for Puerto Rico. Students may wish to organize themselves into small groups and investigate selected aspects of this island nation (e.g., geography, customs, music, tourist spots, etc.). The class may wish to contact a local travel agency and obtain additional brochures, flyers, and tourist information for inclusion in their own publications.

5. Invite students to write a sequel to this story. How can the family best prepare for a future hurricane? What changes or modifications can they make to their home that will help it survive another storm? What kinds of emergency procedures should the family adopt?

6. Invite a representative of the local chapter of the American Red Cross to visit your classroom. Invite him or her to share emergency preparedness procedures as well as rescue operations the Red Cross uses in hurricane situations. The person may wish to recount the efforts of the Red Cross during a recent storm (hurricane).

7. Invite students to each create an illustration or collage of a family working together before, during, or after a natural disaster. If they wish, students may create an imaginary illustration of their own families during a storm or some other catastrophic event. What are the roles and/or obligations of individual family members during such an event? How would family members work together to survive the event?

8. Invite students to gather newspaper and/or magazine articles about weather or bring in information from the daily weather forecasts that are contained in local newspapers or television news shows. Articles can be filed in shoe boxes and shared in a *Weather News* area. Encourage students to examine all the clippings and compile a list comparing and contrasting the different types of forecasts.

9. Discuss why weather is different in different places. How can we find out the weather in the United States? What symbols could we use to record and report the weather on a map? Use the map in your local newspaper to find this information. For homework, have students research the weather patterns of the United States. Make weather symbols from pieces of construction paper and position them on a map of the United States to denote the weather forecast for that particular day. Change these as the conditions in selected areas change.

10. Designate a weatherperson of the day to predict the next day's weather. Invite each student to write his or her prediction on a card and put it on the bulletin board, to be uncovered the next morning. Be sure to talk about the current weather conditions and how they might affect the weather the following day.

11. Many sayings and predictions about the weather have been handed down from one generation to the next. Following are two sayings that have been passed down through the years:

    a. "Red sky at morning—sailor take warning. Red sky at night—sailor's delight."
    b. "A January fog will freeze a hog."

    Invite students to look through other books and assemble a collection of weather sayings that have been handed down through the years. How accurate are those sayings? How do those sayings compare with actual meteorological events?

12. Because people did not always understand the weather, they have held many beliefs about the conditions or situations that caused weather patterns. Following are four beliefs held through the ages:

    a. Sea fog was once thought to be the breath of an underwater monster.
    b. In Germany, some people believed that a cat washed itself just before a rain shower.
    c. The Aztecs believed the sun god could be kept strong and bright only through sacrificing humans.
    d. The Norse thought that weather was created by the god Thor, who raced across the sky in a chariot pulled by two giant goats.

    Invite students to investigate beliefs people have had about hurricanes. They may wish to collect their data from trade books, encyclopedias, or conversations with weather experts. Encourage them to collect these beliefs into a notebook or journal.

13. When a hurricane is predicted for a specific area of the country (e.g., the Gulf Coast, Florida, the eastern seaboard) invite students to track the history of that storm. They may wish to consult the daily newspaper, a weekly newsmagazine, radio and television broadcasts, or first-hand accounts from meteorologists or television weather forecasters. Students can then transfer the "life story" of a hurricane into an album and include a variety of photos and news stories.

14. As a class, students may wish to create a weather dictionary containing all the hurricane words they have learned from their investigations. They may wish to include definitions and illustrations, or to find pictures in magazines or newspapers.

15. Many local television weather forecasters visit elementary classrooms as a regular part of their jobs. Contact your local television station and inquire about scheduling a visit from the local weatherperson. Give students time to prepare questions about hurricanes before the visit.

16. Invite students to discuss and share family adventures, outings, or traditions. You may wish to create a special bulletin board display on which students can regularly post significant occurrences. You may wish to label the bulletin board *Our Family of the Week* and invite each student to contribute memorable photos, artifacts, or other mementos every week for posting on the board. Plan time for students to share their families regularly.

# Smoky Night
## Eve Bunting
(San Diego, CA: Harcourt Brace, 1994)

## Summary

Daniel and his mother look out of their window at the smoky night below. There are looters on the street, fires in the distance, and chaos everywhere. Daniel clutches his cat; but later, when they're forced to leave their apartment building, the cat can't be found. This is a story not just about lost cats, but rather about how people are brought together as a result of terrible events around them.

## Social Studies Disciplines

anthropology, sociology, history, political science

## NCSS Thematic Strands

culture; time, continuity, and change; individual development and identity; individuals, groups, and institutions; civic ideals and practices

## Critical Thinking Questions

1.  Why do you think people riot?

2.  What did you enjoy most about the illustrations? How did they help you appreciate the story?

3.  For you, what would be scary about being in a riot?

4.  If you could talk with Daniel, what would you like to say?

5.  Why did the story end the way it did?

## Related Books

Bunting, Eve. *December.* San Diego, CA: Harcourt Brace, 1997.

———— . *Going Home.* New York: HarperCollins, 1996.

MacMillan, Dianne. *Destination Los Angeles.* Minneapolis, MN: Lerner, 1997.

Miller, Marilyn. *The Bridge at Selma.* New York: Silver Burdett Press, 1989.

Steele, Philip. *Riots: Past and Present.* New York: New Discovery, 1993.

Wisniewski, David. *Golem.* New York: Clarion, 1996.

## *Activities*

1. Invite students to write a sequel to the story. What will happen between Daniel's mother and Mrs. Kim? What will happen between the two cats? How will the neighborhood look? How will the neighborhood be fixed up? Plan time for students to share their endings with each other.

2. This book won the Caldecott Medal in 1995 for its exquisite illustrations. Plan time to talk with students about the illustrations and what they contributed to the book. Invite youngsters to duplicate one or more of the illustrations and/or collages; you may wish to post their renditions on the bulletin board.

3. Eve Bunting is one of this country's most well respected and well known children's authors. Students may wish to obtain information about this popular author at **http://www.friend.ly.net/scoop/biographies/ebunting.html**. Invite students to assemble a biographical sketch of Eve Bunting to contribute to the school library.

4. Invite the school librarian to visit your class with some of Eve Bunting's books. Ask the librarian to read selections from several books. Encourage students to note any similarities between stories. What types of events or themes does she write about most often? Students may wish to assemble a collage (using techniques illustrated in *Smoky Night*) of Eve Bunting's books, characters, or themes.

5. Discuss different types of families with your students. This book portrays a single-parent family. In a comfortable environment, invite students to share the different types of families of which they are a part. Discuss the varieties of families that exist today. Students may wish to create a large class collage of the various family types represented in the classroom. This can be posted on a classroom bulletin board.

6.  Plan time to talk about what makes a family a family. What are the essential ingredients? What are the necessary components? What are the primary elements? Invite students (in small groups) to assemble a *Guide to the Family*. Provide opportunities for them to share their respective guides.

7.  Invite a police officer to visit your classroom (you may want to provide her or him with a copy of *Smoky Night* to read before the visit). Ask the officer to discuss riots, how and why they occur, and the efforts of police officers to control or curtail those events. What special training must police officers have in riot control? What are some of the regulations they must follow?

8.  Invite students to organize themselves into two or three separate groups. Invite each group to mime some of the events in the story for their classmates. Which events are the most significant? Which ones present the greatest challenges for mime? Plan time to talk about the presentations and how they realistically portrayed the story's events or those in a real riot.

9.  Students may enjoy developing the story into a readers theatre script (three examples of readers theatre scripts appear throughout this book). Using the events of the story, a narrator, and selected characters, students may wish to reenact the book for class members or for another class.

10. Invite students to each create a story map, semantic web, or other graphic organizer for the story. Students may wish to work alone or in small groups. Post all the organizers along one wall of the classroom and provide opportunities for students to share their renditions of the book. Which one best captures the mood or intent of the story?

11. Discuss with students different ways, techniques, and methods of resolving conflicts. Why do people get upset with each other in the first place? How can they resolve their differences without resorting to arguing, fighting, or rioting? You may wish to invite the school counselor into your classroom to share some conflict resolution techniques with your students. The class may want to propose some resolution strategies that could have been used to prevent the riots depicted in the book.

12. Just as families are made up of individuals, so too, are neighborhoods and communities. Invite students to discuss what makes a community a community and a neighborhood a neighborhood. What is it about their communities or neighborhoods that make them so special? Students may wish to create an oversized collage of their individual or collective neighborhoods for posting in the classroom or in the school library.

13. Invite students to investigate some of the other children's books that David Diaz has illustrated (your school librarian can help you). What is so distinctive about his illustrations? What do you enjoy most about his work? Students may wish to compose an imaginary letter of appreciation to Mr. Diaz in celebration of his artistic talents and skills.

# Chapter 6

## Community and Neighborhood

### Peter's Place
**Sally Grindley**
(San Diego, CA: Gulliver, 1996)

## Summary

Peter lives in an ecologically rich place full of birds, seals, otters, seaweed, and shore grass. An oil tanker runs aground offshore and spills its cargo on the shore. Peter and his neighbors work tirelessly to rid the coast and its inhabitants of the oil, but only time can erase the scars from their environment.

## Social Studies Disciplines

economics, sociology, geography

## NCSS Thematic Strands

people, places, and environment; production, distribution, and consumption; science, technology, and society

## Critical Thinking Questions

1.  What will be the long-term effects of the oil spill?

2.  Why was Peter so concerned about the eider duck?

3.  Is Peter like you or any of your friends?

4. What can people do to prevent accidents like this from happening?

5. Why does the author write "[the] ugly black scars . . . can never be washed away"?

## Related Books

Chinery, Michael. *Questions and Answers About Seashore Animals.* New York: Kingfisher, 1994.

Fredericks, Anthony D. *Exploring the Oceans: Science Activities for Kids.* Golden, CO: Fulcrum, 1998.

———. *Surprising Swimmers.* Minnetonka, MN: NorthWord Press, 1996.

Guiberson, Brenda. *Into the Sea.* New York: Henry Holt, 1996.

Hare, Tony. *Polluting the Sea.* New York: Gloucester Press, 1991.

Rinard, Judith. *Along a Rocky Shore.* Washington, DC: National Geographic Society, 1990.

Silver, Donald M. *One Small Square: Seashore.* New York: W. H. Freeman, 1993.

## Activities

1. Invite youngsters to keep a watch on the local news or local newspaper for reports of ocean pollution from around the world. Although they may wish to focus on events related to grounded tankers, they can track other types of pollution as well. Invite students to hang up a large wall map of the world. For each incidence of ocean pollution, invite youngsters to write a brief summary (date, nature of occurrence, place, resolution, etc.) on a 3-x-5-inch index card. Post each card around the wall map and connect the card with the actual location on the map using a length of yarn (the yarn can be taped or pinned to the wall).

2. Here's an activity that will give students an opportunity to simulate an ocean in a bottle.

   *Materials*: an empty one-liter soda bottle (with a screw-on top), salad oil, water, blue food coloring

   *Directions*:

   a. Fill an empty one-liter soda bottle 1/3 of the way up with salad oil.
   b. Fill the rest of the bottle (all the way to the brim) with water dyed with a few drops of blue food coloring.
   c. Put on the top securely and lay the bottle on its side.
   d. Now, slowly and gently tip the bottle back and forth.

   The oil in the bottle with begin to roll and move just like the waves in the ocean. Students will have created a miniature ocean in a bottle.

3. Invite students to contact several of the following groups and ask for information on the work they do and the types of printed materials they have available for students:

   American Littoral Society
   Sandy Hook
   Highlands, NJ 07732
   (201-291-0055)

   American Oceans Campaign
   725 Arizona Ave., Suite 102
   Santa Monica, CA 90401
   (310-576-6162)

   Center for Marine Conservation
   1725 DeSales St., NW, Suite 500
   Washington, DC 20036
   (202-429-5609)

   Cetacean Society International
   P.O. Box 953
   Georgetown, CT 06829
   (203-544-8617)

   Coastal Conservation Association
   4801 Woodway, Suite 220 West
   Houston, TX 77056
   (713-626-4222)

The Coral Reef Alliance
809 Delaware St.
Berkeley, CA 94710
(510-528-2492)

International Marine Mammal Project
Earth Island Institute
300 Broadway, Suite 28
San Francisco, CA 94133
(1-800-DOLPHIN)

International Oceanographic Foundation
4600 Rickenbacker Causeway
Virginia Key, Miami, FL 33149
(305-361-4888)

International Wildlife Coalition (IWC) and The Whale Adoption Project
70 E. Falmouth Highway
E. Falmouth, MA 02536
(508-548-8328)

Marine Environmental Research Institute
772 W. End Ave.
New York, NY 10025
(212-864-6285)

Marine Technology Center
1828 L St., NW, Suite 906
Washington, DC 20036-5104
(202-775-5966)

National Coalition for Marine Conservation
3 W. Market St.
Leesburg, VA 20176
(703-777-0037)

National Wildlife Federation
8925 Leesburg Pike
Vienna, VA 22184-0001
(703-790-4000)

Ocean Voice International
P.O. Box 37026
3332 McCarthy Rd.
Ottawa, Ontario, Canada K1V 0W0
(613-990-8819)

4.  The following activity will alert children to the speed at which oil can befoul a seaside community.

    *Directions*: Provide students with four sealable sandwich bags. Label the bags "A," "B," "C," and "D." Fill each bag ⅓ full with water and ⅓ full with used motor oil. Invite students to place a hard-boiled egg in each bag. Seal the bags. Invite students to remove the eggs from each of the bags (they should wear kitchen gloves or some sort of disposable gloves) according to the following schedule:

    from bag A—after 15 minutes
    from bag B—after 30 minutes
    from bag C—after 60 minutes
    from bag D—after 120 minutes

    Encourage students to peel each hard-boiled egg and note the amount of pollution that has seeped through the shell and onto the egg white. Which egg has the most pollution? How rapidly did the pollution seep into each egg? Provide time afterwards to discuss the rapidity with which these eggs became polluted and the implications for spilled oil polluting a beach or shoreline.

5.  Waves constantly pound the shoreline; this has been going on for millions of years. As a result, rocks are broken down through constant wave action. Here's a fun activity that demonstrates this process:

    *Materials*: white glue, playground sand, water, small coffee can (with lid), cookie sheet.

    *Directions*:

    a.  Mix together six tablespoons of white glue with six tablespoons of sand in a bowl.
    b.  Using the tablespoon, place small lumps of the mixture on a cookie sheet.
    c.  Place the cookie sheet in a slow oven (250 degrees) and bake for three to four hours.
    d.  Remove the simulated rocks and allow them to cool.
    e.  Put three or four rocks into a coffee can with some water and place the lid securely on top.
    f.  Shake for four to five minutes and remove the lid.

The rocks will begin to wear down. Eventually all the rocks will be worn down into sand. The action of the simulated waves inside the coffee can causes the rocks to wear against each other. As a result, they break down into smaller and smaller pieces. On a beach or shoreline this process takes many years, but the result is the same. Rocks become smaller by being tossed against each other by the waves. Over time, rocks wear down into particles that eventually become part of the beach or shoreline.

6. Students can build a three-dimensional model of a shoreline or tidal area with the following activity:

   *Materials*: deep baking pan (a bread loaf pan is ideal), nonstick vegetable spray. 4 cups flour, 1 cup salt, 1½ cups of warm water, acrylic or tempera paints.

   *Directions*:

   a. Knead the flour, salt, and warm water together in a large bowl for about 10 minutes (the mixture should be stiff but pliable).

   b. Spray the baking pan with vegetable spray.

   c. Spread the mixture into the pan, forming it into various land forms (beach, rocky shore, sand dunes, outcroppings, cliffs). If necessary, you can make more of the mixture from the same recipe.

   d. Bake at 325 degrees for about one hour or more, depending on size and thickness.

   e. Test the sculpture for "doneness" by sticking a toothpick into various spots (the sculpture should be firm-to-hard). If it is still soft, continue baking until firm.

   f. Remove the sculpture from the oven and allow to cool.

   g. Carefully slide the sculpture from the baking pan (this should be done by an adult).

   h. Paint the sculpture with different colors of acrylic or tempera paints (available at any art, craft, or hobby store).

   *Optional*: When the paint is dry, spray the sculpture with a clear varnish to preserve it.

7. Various organizations publish brochures, leaflets, and guidebooks on ocean pollution and ways to prevent it. Encourage students to write to some of these groups requesting pertinent information. When the resources arrive, plan time to discuss with students methods and procedures in which they can participate to prevent or alleviate this global problem. Invite them to prepare an action plan for themselves and their friends in which they take a proactive stance against ocean pollution. The following will get them started:

   a. The New York Sea Grant Extension Program (125 Nassau Hall, SUNY, Stony Brook, NY 11794-5002 [516-632-8730]) has a free 24-page booklet *Earth Guide: 88 Action Tips for Cleaner Water.*

b.  A variety of informational brochures are available from the NOAA Marine Debris Information Office, Center for Marine Conservation, 1725 DeSales St., NW, Washington, DC 20036.

c.  If students are interested in adopting an endangered animal—specifically a whale, they can write for further information to the International Wildlife Coalition, Whale Adoption Project, 634 North Falmouth Highway, Box 388, North Falmouth, MA 02566.

d.  Invite students to write to the Strathmore Legacy's Eco Amigos Club, 333 Park St., West Springfield, MA 01089; through this group, they can join a coalition of youngsters from around the country who are friendly towards the environment.

e.  Invite students to contact Keep America Beautiful (99 Park Ave., New York, NY 10016) and ask for *Pollution Pointers for Elementary Students*—a list of environment-improvement activities.

8.  The book discusses some of the efforts to contain ocean pollution such as spreading oil. One method is to place a boom (a floating line) in the water in an attempt to contain the oil spill. Students can experiment with different devices to contain their own oil spill and to determine the best material to use in a boom.

   *Directions*: Place water in a large round pan or pie plate. Invite students to collect several different floating objects that could be used as booms (these may include a rubber band; a length of yarn, string, twine, or cotton batting; a ring of Styrofoam cut from the top of a disposable coffee cup, etc. [invite students to use their creative powers in inventing other types of potential booms]). Place several drops of cooking oil in the middle of the water (students will note that because oil and water do not mix, the oil floats on top of the water). Invite students to encircle the oil with one or more different devices to determine which device or which material best prevents the oil from spreading across the surface of the water. To further test their devices, create small ripples in the water of the pan with your finger.

   Invite students to note what happens to the oil on the surface. Take time to discuss the difficulties that arise in the ocean when the surf is high or the seas are rough and oil on the surface must be contained. How do their devices work in containing oil on a choppy simulated sea? What are the implications in real-life rescue efforts?

9.  Invite each student to compose a story about his or her favorite place. Assemble these stories into a class book to be donated to the school library. If you wish, encourage students to speculate on procedures they would use to protect their favorite places or to discuss techniques that could be used to clean up their favorite places should they ever become polluted.

10. Invite students to log on to one or both of the following Web sites: **http://inspire. ospi.wednet.edu:8001.curric/oceans** (this site offers information on a variety of topics—tracking drifter buoys, investigating ocean currents, ocean color, and plant life in the ocean) and **http://seawifs/gsfc.nasa.gov/ocean_planet.html** (this site is a listing of oceanography-related resources that can be found on the Internet.

11. Invite students to interview several of their neighbors and/or relatives. What if an oil spill (e.g., a tanker truck overturning on the highway) occurred in our community or neighborhood, what could we do to clean it up? How could an oil spill be prevented? Invite students to collect and compare the various responses.

12. Invite students to write a sequel to the book—one that takes place five years in the future. What will the local environment look like? What will the long-term effects on the plant and animal life be? What will Peter be doing?

13. Invite students to create a special telephone directory yellow pages for pollution cleanup services, environmental protection groups, and wildlife preservation groups in their local communities or neighborhoods. Encourage students to design the directory as an abbreviated or modified version of the local yellow pages—one that could be a quick and ready resource for community leaders in the event of an environmental crisis.

# The Shaman's Apprentice
## Lynne Cherry and Mark Plotkin
(San Diego, CA: Gulliver, 1998)

## Summary

Deep in the Amazon rainforest a young boy, Kamanya, learns the secrets of the plants of the rainforest from the shaman Nahtahlah. Missionaries come to the village and change the way of life practiced over hundreds of years. But a young woman, in a selfless act of devotion, preserves the ancient rituals and helps Kamanya become the shaman's apprentice and, eventually, the shaman. This story will inspire and excite youngsters as few books do. A wonderful addition to any classroom library and any study of rainforest life.

## Social Studies Disciplines

geography, anthropology, economics, history, sociology

## NCSS Thematic Strands

culture; time, continuity, and change; people, places, and environment; individuals, groups, and institutions; science, technology, and society; global connections

## Critical Thinking Questions

1. How do plants affect your life?

2. What do you think would happen if all the rainforests were eliminated?

3. What can kids do to protect the rainforests?

4. Would you enjoy visiting a rainforest? What would you like to see there?

5. Why do you think the authors decided to write a book about the Amazonian rainforest?

## Related Books

Fredericks, Anthony D. *Clever Camouflagers*. Minnetonka, MN: NorthWord Press, 1997.

———. *Exploring the Rainforest: Science Activities for Kids*. Golden, CO: Fulcrum, 1996.

———. *Simple Nature Experiments with Everyday Materials*. New York: Sterling, 1995.

Gibbons, Gail. *Nature's Green Umbrella*. New York: Morrow Junior Books, 1991.

Pratt, Kristin J. *A Walk Through the Rainforest*. Nevada City, CA: Dawn Publications, 1992.

Silver, Donald M. *Why Save the Rainforest?* New York: Julian Messner, 1993.

Taylor, Barbara. *Rain Forest*. New York: Dorling Kindersley, 1992.
Willow, Diane. *At Home in the Rain Forest*. Watertown, MA: Charlesbridge, 1991.

## *Activities*

1.  Invite students to make a collage of all the plants listed in the book.

2.  Students may wish to look at an extensive rainforest project developed by a group of fourth-grade students at Highland Park Elementary School **http://www.hipark.austin. isd.tenet.edu/home/projects/fourth/rainforests/main.html**.

3.  Invite students to log on to **http://www.mobot.org/MBGnet/sets/rforest/plants/ index.htm** to learn about the various species of plants that live in the world's rainforests.

4.  The Rainforest Action Network provides students with an incredible array of activities and information. Invite your students to log on to their Web site **http://www.ran.org/ran**. Encourage students to share the information learned through a special display in the school library or in a prominent display case.

5.  Visit a local paper recycling center. Be sure to explain to students that if people recycle, millions of trees can be saved (students may be interested in learning that 60,000 trees are needed for just one run of the Sunday *New York Times*). Students may wish to create a campaign for their families on how they and their relatives can recycle.

6.  Invite students to create a large map of Brazil on a bulletin board or on a sheet of newsprint that has been taped to the wall. Encourage them to color in the areas of Brazil that contain rainforests. Allow each student to select one of the plants illustrated in the book, draw it with colored pencils, and attach it to the rainforest area of the map.

7.  Invite students to write a sequel to the story. What will Kamanya do as the shaman? How did he use his knowledge to cure the diseases of his people? How did he pass along his knowledge to a new generation?

8.  Create a rainforest in the classroom. Cover the walls with paper and let students paint the scenes of the rainforest, using vibrant colors. They can paint individual animals directly onto the paper, or create them out of papier-mâché or cardboard, and suspend them from the ceiling with strings. Fashion some of the trees and plants in relief by constructing them out of cardboard; attach them to stand out from the wall.

9.  Invite students to plant terrariums, using an old mayonnaise jar, or other wide-mouth jar, to observe a rainforest in miniature.

    *Directions*: Place a layer of clean gravel on the bottom of the jar, followed by a layer of charcoal and a layer of potting soil. Encourage students to bring in small plant cuttings to plant in their terrariums (try to collect slow-growing plants and mosses).

    Students may also wish to create some tools for their terrariums such as tweezers, chopsticks, cotton swabs, long-handled spoons, and a meat baster. For helpful hints, consult *Exploring the Rainforest: Science Activities for Kids* by Anthony D. Fredericks (see *Related Books* above).

10. The class may wish to adopt an animal. Contact the American Association of Zoological Parks and Aquariums (4550 Montgomery Ave., Suite 940N, Bethesda, MD 20814). Allow the class to decide what type of animal to adopt and draw pictures of the adoptee to display in the room.

11. For a donation of $10.00, *CARE* will plant 30 trees in a rural community in Latin America and teach farmers there the best planting techniques. To raise money for this, you may wish to have your class create a play dramatizing an environmental issue. Invite parents and other community members and ask for donations for the cause.

12. Get permission to plant a tree on the school grounds. Take a field trip to a local nursery to learn about the types of trees available for your area. Invite students to help with the planting and care of the tree. They can keep a class journal, writing about the planting, care, and growth of the tree and how the tree changes through the seasons. They may also want to develop a tree baby book by taking photographs of their tree's first year of growth and describing its first spring, its first leaf, the first picnic beneath the tree, etc.

13. Form an ecology club. Interested students can initiate school and community projects aimed at improving the environment; see *50 Simple Things Kids Can Do to Save the Earth* by John Javna (Kansas City, MO: Andrews and McMeel, 1990) for ideas. Invite local senior citizens to join the club and help with the projects.

14. Invite students to write to one or more of the following organizations requesting information on preserving the world's rainforests:

Children's Rainforest
P.O. Box 936
Lewiston, ME 04240

Rainforest Alliance
65 Bleeker St.
New York, NY 10012-2420

Rainforest Preservation Foundation
P.O. Box 820308
Fort Worth, TX 76182

Save the Rainforest
604 Jamie St.
Dodgeville, WI 53533

15. Invite students to take a field trip through their houses to locate various products obtained from the rainforest. Some of the raw materials obtained from the rainforest and used in many home products are acids, alcohols, balsa wood, bamboo, camphor, chicle, citronella, dyes, fibers, flavorings, hemp, kapok, latexes, mahogany, oils, palms, rattan, resins, rubber, spices, sweeteners, teak, and waxes.

16. Invite students to interview their family doctors or local pharmacists about rainforest drugs used in the treatment of selected diseases and illnesses. Here is an abbreviated list:

| Disease | Medicine |
| --- | --- |
| malaria | quinine |
| nervous disorders | reserpine |
| leukemia | vincristine |
| heart disease | digitalis |
| tetanus | curare |
| arthritis | cortisone |

17. Explain to students that all plants, including rainforest plants, grow toward a light source. Here's an experiment that demonstrates how powerful that process is; you'll need a small potted plant with a strong root system, two large sponges, and string.

*Directions*:

a. Carefully remove the plant from its pot. Try to leave as much soil around the roots as possible.

b. Wet the sponges and wrap them around the root system as in the illustration. Tie the sponges together with string.

    c.    Turn the plant upside down (the roots will be on the top) and, using a string or wire hanger, hang it from the ceiling near a window where there is lots of sunlight.

    d.    Check the plant occasionally and keep the sponges moistened.

The leaves and stems of plants will grow in the direction of a light source. This process is known as *phototropism*. The roots will grow downward to reach the necessary nutrients in the soil.

18.    Students may wish to grow some rainforest plants right in their own classroom. Invite them to visit a large supermarket, garden shop, or nursery and look for one or more of the following rainforest plants: African violet, begonia, bird's-nest fern, bromeliad, Christmas cactus, corn plant, croton, dumb cane, fiddle-leaf fig, orchid, philodendron, prayer plant, rubber plant, snake plant, umbrella plant, and zebra plant. Inform students that the plants they grow in the classroom will be somewhat smaller than the plants normally found throughout the rainforest.

19.    You and your students may wish to adopt an acre of tropical rainforest land. For a donation of $35.00, your class will receive an honorary land deed, a detailed description of the adopted acreage, a colorful decal, and reports from the field. Raise the money through a classroom fund-raising project or through a donation from the Home and School Association. Contact the Nature Conservancy's *Adopt an Acre Program* (4245 N. Fairfax Drive, Arlington, VA 22203 [1-800-84-ADOPT]).

# *The Summer My Father Was Ten*

## Pat Brisson

(Honesdale, PA: Boyds Mills Press, 1998)

## *Summary*

This is a touching story about trust and responsibility. It tells of the bond built between an old man and a young boy—a boy who unwittingly destroys one of the most sacred things in the old man's life: his garden. With affecting prose and a delightful insight into the feelings of youngsters and the sensibilities of old men, the author weaves a timeless tale that will spark wonderful discussions in any classroom.

## *Social Studies Disciplines*

sociology, history

## *NCSS Thematic Strands*

time, continuity, and change; individual development and identity; power, authority, and governance; civic ideals and practices

## *Critical Thinking Questions*

1. If you were the young boy in the story, would you have done the same thing he did?

2. Was the old man similar to anyone you know in your family?

3. What was the "lesson" the narrator learned from her father?

4. Why didn't the boy's friends help him when he worked with the old man on the garden?

5. Have you ever done something to someone and felt ashamed about it? How did you deal with that incident?

6. If you could write a letter to the father, what would you say?

## *Related Books*

Drake, Jane. *The Kids Summer Games Book*. Toronto: Kids Can Press, 1998.

Fredericks, Anthony D. *Simple Nature Experiments with Everyday Materials*. New York: Sterling, 1995.

Herck, Alice. *The Enchanted Gardening Book*. New York: Random House, 1997.

Lipsyte, Robert. *One Fat Summer*. New York: HarperCollins, 1991.

MacLachlan, Patricia. *Journey*. New York: Delacorte, 1991.

Rosen, Michael. *Down to Earth: Garden Secrets! Garden Stories! Garden Projects You Can Do!* San Diego, CA: Harcourt Brace, 1998.

Talmage, Ellen. *Container Gardening for Kids.* New York: Sterling, 1997.

## *Activities*

1. Invite students to conduct an imaginary interview with the father in the story. Invite one student to take the role of the father. Encourage one or more other students to interview the father about his memories or perceptions of the event depicted in the book. If possible, you may wish to videotape the interview.

2. Invite students to write a series of imaginary diary entries as though they were taking on the persona of Mr. Bellavista. How would he have recorded his perceptions or feelings about the tomato-throwing incident? How did he feel? What did he want to do with the boys? Encourage students to share their various diary entries with each other.

3. Students will enjoy the following creative activity:

   *Directions*: Invite a student to fill a flat cake pan with soil. Smooth the soil so that it is level. Moisten it lightly with water and, using the end of a toothpick or the tip of a knife, trace the student's name lightly into the soil.

   Open a package of radish seeds and carefully plant the seeds in the grooves made for the letters of the student's name (encourage the student to follow the directions on the seed packet for proper planting depth and distance between seeds). Cover the seeds with soil and pat down lightly. Place the pan in a sunny location and water occasionally. After a few days the seeds will sprout into the shape of the student's name.

   Invite other students to repeat this activity with their own pans of soil. Students may also wish to use different types of vegetables (e.g., parsley, mung) or flower or grass seeds. Which varieties yield the prettiest names? Which varieties yield the most decorative or unusual names?

4. What conditions do seeds need to germinate? The following experiment can help students discover the answer to that question:

   *Directions*: Invite students to label each of six sealable sandwich bags with a number from 1 to 6. Cut three paper towels in half, moisten three pieces and place a piece in the bottom of each of three sandwich bags. Drop six radish seeds in each of the six bags and continue setting up all the bags as follows:

   Bag #1: seeds, moist paper towel, no light (put in a closet or drawer), room temperature

   Bag #2: seeds, moist paper towel, light, room temperature

   Bag #3: seeds, dry paper towel, light, room temperature

   Bag #4: seeds, no paper towel, water (seeds floating), light, room temperature

   Bag #5: seeds, moist paper towel, no light, place in refrigerator or freezer

Bag #6: seeds, moist paper towel, no light, room temperature, seeds covered with nail polish

Invite students to record the date and time they started the activity and to check each bag twice daily for two to three weeks. Changes should be recorded in a journal or notebook. Invite students to make conclusions about the conditions necessary for seeds to germinate.

5.  Invite students to create a prequel or sequel to the story. What could have taken place before the story began? What could have happened after the story concluded? Encourage students to discuss differences or changes they might add to the story if the author had invited them to do so. Students may wish to speculate that they are related to Mr. Bellavista. How would that affect the events that could happen before or after the book's story?

6.  Invite students to look in the local telephone yellow pages and create a list of the services Mr. Bellavista might have needed for his garden. For example, a nursery, a clothing store, a doctor (for bee stings), and a bookstore (for gardening guides). Invite students to suggest other possibilities. Encourage them to create a special set of yellow pages designed especially for Mr. Bellavista (information can be prepared with a word processing program and duplicated on sheets of yellow paper). Students can share the bound book among themselves.

7.  Invite students to initiate a chart similar to the one below (see table 6.1). Encourage them to add to the items already included on the list with the aid of library resources. Take time to discuss the various uses plants have in your own life, your family life, or around the house. Students can add to this chart throughout the school year.

**Table 6.1. How We Use Plants**

| Food | Medicine | Industrial Products | Home Products |
|------|----------|---------------------|---------------|
| cocoa | quinine | rubber | lumber |
| cinnamon | | dyes | paper |
| maple syrup | | | |
| tomatoes | | | |
| onions | | | |

8. Invite students to obtain a piece of cardboard (approximately 8½-x-11 inches). Cut a rectangle out of the center, leaving a border of approximately 1½ inches. Encourage them to hold the cardboard border at arm's length to frame a nearby plant (perhaps a vegetable). What do they see? Where is the light? What does the sky look like behind the plant? Is the plant wider than it is tall? Does it resemble a triangle, a square, a rectangle, or a circle?

   Taking their observations into consideration, encourage them to talk about how they might illustrate that plant. Provide them with simple materials (crayons, paper, etc.) and invite them to draw a rendition of their plant. Do they see a tomato plant differently from the illustrator of this book? How differently? Take time to discuss any differences or similarities. What differences or similarities in illustrations exist between and among a group of children (e.g., choice of plant, drawing style, color)?

9. Obtain two similar potted plants (of equal vigor and height). Invite students to select 20 random leaves from one plant. Ask students to smear a thin layer of petroleum jelly on the tops of 10 leaves and on the bottoms of 10 other leaves (on the same plant). Place both plants on a window sill and water and fertilize as necessary. Several days later, invite students to observe the two plants and note the differences. What happened to the leaves with petroleum jelly on the top? What happened to the leaves with petroleum jelly on the bottom? What can this tell us about some of the processes of plants?

10. Obtain two similar potted plants (of equal vigor and height). Water and fertilize the plants as necessary. Invite one student to place a large clear cellophane bag over the top of one plant and secure it around the pot with a rubber band (the bag should be as airtight as possible around the plant). Place the plants on a window sill. Several days later, encourage students to note what is happening inside the bagged plant. Students may wish to remove the bag from that plant occasionally and measure the amount of water transpired from the plant (every two days, for example). Be sure to water both plants adequately.

11. Invite students to complete one or more of the following sentence stems:

    "If I were the narrator, I would . . ."
    "If I were Mr. Bellavista, I would . . ."
    "If I were the young boy, I would . . ."
    "If I were the grandmother, I would . . ."
    "If I were one of the boy's friends, I would . . ."

    Plan time for students to discuss how they would complete each of the stems. You may wish to let students know that there are no right or wrong responses to this activity.

12. Invite students to talk about the roles and responsibilities of neighbors. What is a neighbor? What does a neighbor do for others in her or his community? What makes a neighborhood a neighborhood? What do students like (or dislike) about their neighborhoods?

13. Invite students to design a neighborhood questionnaire. Students may wish to interview their neighbors on what they think makes a good neighborhood. How are the perceptions of adults different from (or similar to) the perceptions of students? Encourage students to create a chart, graph, or mural that defines the essential ingredients of a good neighborhood.

14. Invite students to create a community newspaper. Students may wish to create current-event articles on the local neighborhood, a series of community cartoons, a sports page, movie and play reviews and schedules, PTO meetings, etc. Students who live in the same neighborhood can rotate assignments (sports reporter, fashion editor, etc.).

15. You may wish to initiate a simulation on the creation of a new neighborhood. Divide the class into small groups and invite them to respond to the following questions:

    a. Where will the new neighborhood be located?
    b. What kinds of buildings will be in the new neighborhood?
    c. What kinds of resources or supplies must be taken to the new neighborhood?
    d. How many people will live in the new neighborhood?
    e. What kinds of people do you want in your neighborhood?
    f. What rules or laws must be set up in your new neighborhood?

    When each group has generated some responses to those questions, invite them to decide how they will handle one of the following challenges to their new neighborhood: a) a group of tough guys moves into the neighborhood; b) the town council decides to evict everyone over 65; c) residents want a new park for their children to play in; or d) a vacant lot will be turned into a community garden.

16. Celebrate a Neighborhood Day in your classroom. Invite various people from your community to visit and share information about their occupations. You may choose to invite the mayor, the fire chief, the postmaster, a doctor, a nurse, the owner of the lumber store, a sanitation worker, a seamstress, an insurance salesperson, or representatives of other occupational groups. Provide a forum in which students can interview each of the visitors and collect the data in the form of a scrapbook or a series of brochures.

17. Schedule a Neighborhood of the Week. Each week, invite students to bring in photographs of their neighborhoods, listings of neighborhood events, special attractions, or unusual buildings. They can prepare descriptions and captions for each of these and then post them on the bulletin board.

18. Invite students to write journal entries about one thing in their own neighborhoods they would like to change. Why did they select that particular item? How would they change it? How would that change benefit other neighborhood residents?

# The Village of Round and Square Houses

## Ann Grifalconi

(Boston: Little, Brown, 1986)

## Summary

In the Cameroons of Central Africa exists an isolated village named Tos. In that village the women live in round houses and the men live in square houses. The story of how this came to be is told through the eyes of a young girl as she shares a beautiful legend about a community and its people.

## Social Studies Disciplines

geography, anthropology, sociology, history

## NCSS Thematic Strands

culture; time, continuity, and change; people, places, and environment; individuals, groups, and institutions; science, technology, and society; global connections; civic ideals and practices

## Critical Thinking Questions

1. How is the village of Tos similar to the town or city in which you live?

2. What did you enjoy most about life in the village of Tos (before the volcano erupted)?

3. How is the narrator similar to you, to a family member, or to one of your friends?

4. How do such natural events as erupting volcanoes and earthquakes change the way people live?

5. How would your life change if a volcano erupted nearby?

## Related Books

Arnott, Kathleen. *African Myths and Legends*. New York: Oxford University Press, 1990.

Ayo, Yvonne. *Africa*. New York: Alfred A. Knopf, 1995.

Lauber, Patricia. *Volcano: The Eruption and Healing of Mount St. Helens*. New York: Bradbury Press, 1986.

Musgrove, Margaret. *Ashanti to Zulu*. New York: Dial Press, 1992.

Onyefulu, Ifeoma. *Chidi Only Likes Blue: An African Book of Colors*. New York: Cobblehill, 1997.

Petersen, David. *Africa*. New York: Watts, 1998.

Simon, Seymour. *Volcanoes*. New York: Mulberry, 1988.

Taylor, Barbara. *Mountains and Volcanoes*. New York: Kingfisher, 1993.

Watt, Fiona. *Earthquakes and Volcanoes*. London: Usborne, 1993.

## *Activities*

1.  Invite students to complete some of the sentence stems below:

    "If I lived in Africa, I would . . ."

    "If my family lived in round/square houses, we would . . ."

    "If I were the young girl (in the story), I would . . ."

    "If I lived in a small village, I . . ."

    "If I lived near a volcano, I . . ."

2.  Obtain copies of several different telephone books. Invite students to browse through the yellow pages and locate items or services that might be needed in the event of a local volcanic eruption (e.g., telephone service, carpet cleaning, home repair). Students may wish to create their own special *Volcano Yellow Pages* listing services that are not normally found in most municipal phone books (e.g., lava removal, air purification, etc.).

3.  Students may wish to create their own chemical volcano. They can participate in the gathering and setup of materials. This activity, however, should be done under adult supervision only.

    *Materials*: empty soda bottle, liquid detergent, red food coloring, vinegar, warm water, baking soda.

    *Directions*: Set an empty soda bottle on the ground or in the sand of a playground sandbox. Mound up the dirt or sand around the bottle so that only the top of the neck shows. Pour one tablespoon of liquid detergent into the bottle. Add a few drops of red food coloring, one cup of vinegar, and enough warm water to fill the bottle almost to the top. Very quickly, add two tablespoons of baking soda to the bottle. (The baking soda can be mixed with a little water beforehand. This will make it easier to pour it into the bottle without spilling.) The "volcano" will begin erupting almost immediately. The chemical reaction that occurs between the vinegar and baking soda (which produces large amounts of carbon dioxide gas) will cause the liquid mixture to expand and froth up and out of the bottle top. It will flow out of the bottle and down the sides of the "volcano." (*Note*: This simulation is similar to Hawaiian volcanoes, which ooze lava, as opposed to Plinean volcanoes, which are explosive in nature—as was the one in the story.) The addition of the liquid detergent produces lots of bubbles, and the food color gives the mixture a distinctive color. This "eruption" will last for several minutes. Afterward, invite students to log on to **http://volcano.und.nodak.edu** to compare and contrast different types of volcanoes from around the world.

4. If possible, obtain a copy of either of the following two videos, which are available from the National Geographic Society (Washington, DC): *This Changing Planet* (catalog 30352) or *The Violent Earth* (catalog 51234). Provide opportunities for youngsters to share the similarities and differences between the volcanoes shown in the films and the volcano described in the book.

5. Provide students with copies of different newspapers from selected cities around the country. (Many metropolitan areas have newsstands at which different newspapers from various cities are sold.) Invite students to look through those newspapers for articles, information, or data relating to eruptions of volcanoes (at the time of this writing, Mount Kilauea volcano in Hawaii is in a constant state of eruption). Invite students to cut out those articles and assemble them into an ongoing journal. Index cards with a brief summary of the date, location, and events surrounding an eruption can be posted around a large wall map for others to read.

6. Invite students to create a brief five-minute skit or a short one-act play about the village and villagers both before and after the eruption of the volcano. Encourage them to consider the roles and occupations of both men and women before the eruption and how those roles may have changed after the eruption. What customs or traditions might have remained the same? Which ones might have changed as a result of the men living in one type of house and the women in another? Children may wish to create a short dialogue between two or three characters (men *and* women) that could have taken place before the eruption and another dialogue for those same characters after the eruption. Plan time to discuss any changes in behavior, attitudes, or relationships that may or may not have existed between men and women after the eruption.

7.  Obtain a copy of one of the volcano books listed above and provide opportunities for students to read it. Afterwards, invite students to compare the photographs in *The Village of Round and Square Houses* with volcano photos in other books. Encourage students to categorize the photos from various sources according to one of the four types of volcanoes: shield volcanoes, cinder cone volcanoes, composite volcanoes, and dome volcanoes. Invite children to categorize the volcano in *The Village of Round and Square Houses* into one of the four groups.

8.  Invite students to complete a chart similar to the one below (see table 6.2). Ask them to note any similarities in the customs, traditions, or behaviors of men and women in their town or city to the customs of men and women in the village of Tos. Provide opportunities for youngsters to discuss those comparisons.

**Table 6.2. Comparisons of Men's and Women's Customs**

|  | Customs—Men | Customs—Women |
|---|---|---|
| Tos |  |  |
| My Town |  |  |

9.  Invite students to create illustrations of their own homes. How are their houses or dwellings similar to or different from the houses illustrated in the book? What makes their dwellings unique? What makes the dwellings in the book unique?

10. Organize students into several small groups. Invite each group to investigate the different types of houses used throughout the world. You may want to assign a continent to each of the groups and encourage each group to build scale models of representative houses from various countries and/or cultures within that continent.

11. Invite students to collect newspaper and/or magazine articles about Cameroon. Students may wish to assemble these into an attractive notebook or colorful bulletin board display in the school library. Additional information on this country (and surrounding countries) can be obtained at the following Web sites:

    **http://hyperion.advanced.org/16645/**

    **http://www.hmnet.com/africa/1africa.html**

    **http://www.geographica.com/indx06.htm**

12. Invite students to take an imaginary trip to Cameroon. Encourage them to keep journals about their travels. They may wish to include information such as location, sites, weather, customs, food, and the people. Invite students to note both similarities and differences between the United States and Cameroon.

# Chapter 7

## City and Country

## Bridges Are to Cross

**Philemon Sturges**
(New York: G. P. Putnam's Sons, 1998)

### Summary

Feast your eyes on these bridges from around the world, all painstakingly created with intricately cut paper. They represent the most simple (a log across a river) to the most complex (the Golden Gate Bridge). But bridges represent more than ways to cross water; they reflect our values and lifestyles throughout history. This book shares the wonders of bridges as symbols, celebrations, and solutions.

### Social Studies Disciplines

geography, sociology, political science, economics, history

### NCSS Thematic Strands

culture; time, continuity, and change; people, places, and environment; individuals, groups, and institutions; science, technology, and society; civic ideals and practices

### Critical Thinking Questions

1. Which of the bridges in this book did you most enjoy?

2. Which of the bridges would you most enjoy crossing?

3. What are some of the reasons people build bridges?

4. What is the most spectacular bridge you have crossed?

5. Why are there so many different styles of bridges throughout the world?

6. Why are bridges important to people who live in a city?

## *Related Books*

Doherty, Craig. *The Golden Gate Bridge*. New York: Blackbirch, 1995.

Hunter, Ryan. *Cross a Bridge*. New York: Holiday House, 1998.

Oxlade, Chris. *Bridges*. Austin, TX: Steck-Vaughn, 1997.

———. *Bridges and Tunnels*. New York: Watts, 1994.

Ricciuti, Edward. *America's Top Ten Bridges*. New York: Blackbirch, 1998.

Richardson, Joy. *Bridges*. New York: Watts, 1994.

## *Activities*

1. Your students may enjoy looking at more bridges from around the world: where they are located, how they were constructed, and their specific dimensions. Here are some wonderful Web sites that will provide students with lots of information:

   **http://hyperion.advanced.org/23378/**

   **http://www.pbs.org/wgbh/nova/bridge/**

   **http://www.xs4all.nl/~hnetten/index.html**

2. One of the world's most famous bridges (and one of the bridges featured in this book) is the Golden Gate Bridge in San Francisco. The Web site **http://events.exploratorium.edu/CAM2/index.html** offers students a real time video (updated every few seconds) of the Golden Gate Bridge.

3. Divide the class into several small groups and assign one of the countries mentioned in the book to each group. Encourage each group to investigate library resources and compile a descriptive brochure or newsletter about their assigned country. Students may wish to gather relevant information from a local travel agency to compliment their library gatherings.

4. Invite students to construct a bulletin board display that presents the various types of bridges profiled in this book. Are some types of bridges specific to certain types of countries? With additional library research, students may wish to compile a list of famous bridges from around the world and create an appropriate bulletin board display, too.

5. Invite students to participate in one or more of the following bridge-building activities. Plan enough time for students to discuss the challenges they faced in constructing their bridges as well as those the construction workers might have encountered when building the bridges profiled in the book.

*Paper Structures*: Invite students to take a sheet of newspaper and roll it from one corner to the opposite diagonal corner (keep the newspaper rolled as tightly as possible). At the end, tape the newspaper roll together. Encourage students to continue building a series of newspaper logs. Invite students to construct one or more bridges with their logs. Which rules of geometry contribute to the construction?

*Marshmallow Structures*: Provide student teams with a box of wooden toothpicks and a bag of miniature marshmallows. Invite them to construct the following, using the toothpicks as beams and the marshmallows as glue:

    a.   Invite students to build the tallest structure possible from nine miniature marshmallows and 15 toothpicks.

    b.   Have them build a structure from nine toothpicks and 15 miniature marshmallows. Is it stronger than the first structure? What contributes to its strength?

    c.   Can they create a structure from 14 miniature marshmallows and 20 toothpicks that is strong enough to support a book?

    d.   Invite them to build a bridge between two tables (one foot apart) that will support a stack of four quarters.

*Spaghetti Structures*: Provide students with raw spaghetti and masking tape. Invite them to create one or more of the following:

- a. What is the tallest free-standing structure students can create with only 50 sticks of raw spaghetti?
- b. What is the strongest structure possible between two tables with 50 (or fewer) sticks of spaghetti as building materials? The bridge must be able to hold a weight for a minimum of six seconds (place a container on top and gradually add sand or clay until the structure collapses; afterwards, weigh the container's contents).
- c. What is the longest unsupported structure students can create with 50 sticks of spaghetti? One end must be secured to the end of a table; the other end must not touch any other object.

6. Invite students to experiment with cut paper collages. Provide them with scissors and sheets of construction paper. Encourage them to create cut paper replicas of familiar things (e.g., their houses, a community building, a store). You may wish to challenge some students to duplicate one of the structures illustrated in the book (or a portion of that structure). This activity will challenge many students—plan time to discuss some of the challenges they faced as well as some of the challenges the illustrator must have encountered in designing the bridges in the book.

7. Invite students to interview their parents, grandparents, relatives, or neighbors about some of the bridges they remember best. What bridges have they crossed? Where were some of those bridges located? What city, state, or country had the most bridges? Do they recall any memorable event that occurred on a bridge? Students may wish to assemble their data into a classroom display or tabletop book for the classroom library.

8. Invite students to post an oversize map of the world on one wall of the classroom. Invite them to draw a replica of each of the bridges profiled in the book. They can then post each illustration on the perimeter of the map and string lines of yarn from the illustrations to the specific locations on the world map.

9. Invite students to create the perfect bridge. Invite them to imagine what the ideal bridge would look like and to use some of the ideas in the book as a guide. How might it be constructed? Where would it be located? What would it look like? Encourage each student to illustrate her or his bridge and then share it with the class.

10. Invite students to construct a time line of bridges along one wall of the classroom. Beginning with examples cited in the book, invite students to post illustrations and descriptions of various bridges throughout history. What do they notice about bridge design over time? How has the purpose and function of bridges changed through the years? What do we know about bridge building today that wasn't known or incorporated into bridges many years ago?

11. Encourage students to create a bridge of the future. What will it look like? How will it be built? Students may wish to work together in small teams to design and illustrate a futuristic bridge.

12. Invite students to create an informational booklet about bridges that do not span bodies of water. What are examples of bridges from around the world that are not used to transport people (or machines) across water? How are they used?

13. Invite students to investigate natural bridges—those created by nature (such as Window Rock in Arizona). Where are some natural bridges located? How are they created? Why are they so awe-inspiring? How are they similar to or different from man-made bridges?

14. Encourage students to create a world record book about bridges. They may want to look up and provide information on the following:

> What is the world's oldest bridge?
>
> What is the world's longest bridge?
>
> What is the world's most expensive bridge?
>
> What is the world's tallest bridge?
>
> What is the world's shortest bridge?
>
> What is the world's most unusual bridge?

# *Buffalo Sunrise*

**Diane Swanson**

(San Francisco: Sierra Club Books for Children, 1996)

## Summary

This is a marvelous book about a marvelous creature—the American buffalo. Through stories, old photographs, delightful sidebars, and incredible records, the author has created a tale that is sure to grasp the attention of every youngster. Filled with amazing facts woven into magical prose, this book will become an essential element of any American history unit. A treasure for any classroom!

## Social Studies Disciplines

geography, anthropology, sociology, economics, history

## NCSS Thematic Strands

culture; time, continuity, and change; people, places, and environment; production, distribution, and consumption; global connections

## Critical Thinking Questions

1.  What was the most amazing thing you discovered about the buffalo?

2.  How can people preserve the small herds of buffalo that still exist in this country?

3.  Why are the bald eagle and the buffalo the two best-known symbols of this country?

4.  Which of the illustrations in the book do you feel best depicts the buffalo?

5.  Why were buffalo so revered and prized by Native Americans?

## Related Books

Bellville, Cheryl. *American Bison*. Minneapolis, MN: Carolrhoda, 1992.
Crewe, Sabrina. *The Buffalo*. Austin, TX: Steck-Vaughn, 1997.
Hamilton, John. *Buffalo Bill Cody*. New York: Abdo and Daughters, 1996.
Lepthien, Emilie. *Buffalo*. New York: Children's Press, 1989.
Patent, Dorothy Hinshaw. *Buffalo: The American Bison Today*. New York: Clarion, 1993.
Sanford, William. *Buffalo Bill Cody: Showman of the Wild West*. New York: Enslow, 1996.
Wilkenson, Todd. *Bison for Kids*. Minnetonka, MN: NorthWord Press, 1994.
Wittman, Patricia. *Buffalo Thunder*. New York: Marshall Cavendish, 1997.

## *Activities*

1.  Students may be interested in obtaining additional information about the American bison. They can do so at the following Web sites:

    **http://www.oaklandzoo.org/atoz/azbison.html**

    **http://www-nais.ccm.emr.ca/schoolnet/issues/risk/mammals/emammal/ wdbison.html**

2.  The bison in Yellowstone National Park are being systematically killed and/or removed to preserve the dwindling herds. There are arguments for and against this practice. Students may be interested in researching both sides of the controversy by logging on to the following Web sites:

    **http://www.desktop.org/gyc/bisonwinter.html**

    **http://www.npca.org/yell-bis.html**

    **http://www.desktop.org/gyc/migrations.html**

3.  Divide the class into several small groups and invite each group to take either a *pro* or *con* position on the systematic killing or removal of bison from Yellowstone Park. What are the advantages? What are the disadvantages? Provide each group with an opportunity to argue their position(s).

4.  See page 19 of the book for a list of how the Blackfeet Indians used the buffalo: from its hide to its horns to its organs. Invite students to investigate other animals and the various ways in which they are used in modern society. Which animal has the most uses? Are any animals completely useless? (The hagfish is one that gets my vote.)

5.  Invite students to put together a time line of significant events in the history of the American bison. Encourage students to work in small groups and post a large sheet of newsprint along one wall of the classroom. They may wish to record important dates, personal illustrations, or milestones in the natural history of the bison. Plan time for students to share their creations.

6.  Encourage students to create a shape book. Invite them to cut out an outline of a buffalo from two sheets of oaktag. Students may wish to staple several blank sheets of paper between the two outlines to form a book and then record significant facts, features, or characteristics about buffalo. They can donate these books to the school library.

7.  Schedule a Buffalo Day in your classroom and invite other classes to join the festivities. Students can present skits on Indian life, construct posters or dioramas about buffalo, share stories and folk tales about life on the plains, and construct clay model replicas of various buffalo. Buffalo Day can be a day to celebrate the significance and importance of buffalo through books, stories, songs, and various activities.

8.  Animals live in a variety of environments. Invite children to obtain a journal or notebook and keep an ongoing record of the different types of environments in which local animals live. They may wish to take a field trip throughout their own neighborhood or town or conduct research in the school or public library. For example, they may wish to construct a chart similar to the one below (see table 7.1) and add to it throughout the school year.

**Table 7.1. Animal Habitats**

|  | States | Resident Animals |
| --- | --- | --- |
| Desert |  |  |
| Prairie |  |  |
| Wetlands |  |  |
| Everglades |  |  |
| Tundra |  |  |
| Seashore |  |  |
| Rainforest |  |  |

Invite youngsters to create another chart and investigate the wide variety of environments in which people around the world live. Provide time to discuss the similarities and/or differences between environments in this country and those in other countries. What are the similarities and/or differences?

The activities above can be further extended by inviting children to discuss the similarities between human and animal environments. What are some of the things that determine where an animal lives? Are those conditions or features similar to the considerations of humans in selecting a living site? Invite youngsters to create a chart of the various types of animal homes (e.g., cave, tunnel, hole, nest, ledge, etc.) and examples of the animals that might live in or on those spaces. Do animals have more options for living spaces than humans?

9. Invite children to practice walking like a buffalo (Invite them to walk on their hands and feet). Encourage them to walk around the room in this position. What difficulties do they note? How is their walking similar to or different from the way a real buffalo walks? What problems might they encounter if they had to walk in this manner for most of the day? Afterwards, invite children to conduct library research on the many different ways that animals walk through their respective environments. How does an animal's form of locomotion help it obtain food or survive in its specific environment?

10. Students can learn more about buffalo by obtaining copies of or subscribing to various children's magazines. The list below provides you with some of the most popular children's periodicals devoted to animals. All are available at most school and public libraries.

*Audubon Adventure*
National Audubon Society
613 Riversville Rd.
Greenwich, CT 06830

*Chickadee*
Young Naturalist Foundation
P.O. Box 11314
Des Moines, IA 50340

*Dolphin Log*
Cousteau Society
8430 Santa Monica Blvd.
Los Angeles, CA 90069

*Naturescope*
National Wildlife Federation
1912 16th St., NW
Washington, DC 20036

*Ranger Rick*
National Wildlife Federation
1412 16th St., NW
Washington, DC 20036

*Zoobooks*
Wildlife Education, Ltd.
930 West Washington St.
San Diego, CA 92103

11.   Invite students to write to one or more of the following environmental agencies to obtain relevant literature on buffalo or other endangered species around the world. When the material arrives, invite children to make lists of animals that are the most seriously imperiled, that are endangered, and that are threatened. Invite children to post their lists (which can also be turned into an informative fact sheet or brochure to be shared with others) in the school or some other public building in town.

National Wildlife Federation
8925 Leesburg Pike
Vienna, VA 22184

National Audubon Society
666 Pennsylvania Ave., SE
Washington, DC 20003

Friends of Wildlife Conservation
New York Zoological Society
185 St., Southern Blvd.
Bronx Zoo
Bronx, NY 10460

12.   Provide students with a map of the United States and invite them to plot the locations of the major herds of buffalo in this country. Students may wish to use multiple colors of pencil or chalk to denote the numbers of buffalo 200 years ago, 100 years ago, 50 years ago, and today.

13.   Invite students to create an imaginary book about the life of a buffalo as told from the perspective of the buffalo. The narrator can outline her or his daily life or present details about her or his entire life. Students may wish to have the narrator reflect on how it was in "the good old days" when there was a plethora of buffalo on the plains.

14.   Invite students to write letters to their representatives of Congress on the value of preserving the buffalo. Invite them to ask about any current or pending legislation related to preserving buffalo herds. Students may also elect to write letters to the editor of the local newspaper.

15.   One of the meals the Plains Indians made with buffalo meat was *pemmican*. Your students may enjoy making and tasting this traditional food. (*Note*: Because buffalo meat is not easily obtained in all parts of the country, dried beef has been substituted in this recipe.)

## PEMMICAN

- ✓ 2 pounds of dried beef (or buffalo meat, if available)
- ✓ 1 cup of raisins
- ✓ suet (available from any butcher)

Cut the dried beef into small chunks and place into a meat grinder with the raisins. Grind together until well mixed. Put the mixture on a cookie sheet. Melt the suet in a small pan over medium heat. Pour the suet over the meat until covered. Stir the mixture together and flatten with the back of a large spoon or a rolling pin. Allow to cool and cut into squares (serves 12).

# The Summer Sands
## Sherry Garland
### (San Diego, CA: Gulliver, 1995)

## Summary

This is a delightful story about two children who vacation at their grandfather's house on the shore. Each year, however, winter storms erode the sand dunes they love so much. Neighbors and friends band together to solve an ecological problem with creativity and fortitude. This book celebrates the concept of community effort and the value of neighbors working together. Spanning both social studies *and* science, this is a book to share with all children.

## Social Studies Disciplines

geography, sociology, economics

## NCSS Thematic Strands

time, continuity, and change; people, places, and environment; individuals, groups, and institutions; civic ideals and practices

## Critical Thinking Questions

1.  What did you enjoy most about this story?

2.  How is the area in which the two children vacationed similar to or different from where you live?

3.  Why was it important for the neighbors to preserve the sand dunes?

4.  What might have happened if the sand dunes had not been preserved?

5.  What are some ways in which your neighbors have worked together for a common cause?

## Related Books

Burnie, David. *Seashore*. New York: DK, 1997.
Cooney, Barbara. *Hattie and the Wild Waves*. New York: Viking, 1990.
Levine, Evan. *Not the Piano, Mrs. Medley!* New York: Orchard, 1991.
McMillan, Bruce. *A Beach for the Birds*. New York: Houghton Mifflin, 1993.
Potter, Jean. *Science in Seconds at the Beach*. New York: John Wiley, 1998.
Silver, Donald. *One Small Square: Seashore*. New York: W. H. Freeman, 1993.

## *Activities*

1. Invite students to write a prequel or sequel to this story. What could have taken place before the story begins? What will happen after the story? Provide opportunities for students to share their stories with each other.

2. The author's note at the end of the story provides information on how Texas is preserving its beaches. Invite students to write to the Coastal Conservation Association (4801 Woodway, Suite 220 West, Houston, TX 77056 [1-713-626-4222]) and request information or printed resources on their efforts to preserve the Texas shoreline.

3. The Surfrider Foundation USA is a nonprofit organization dedicated to protecting the coastal environment of California beaches. Your students may wish to log on to their Web site **http://www.surfrider.org** and obtain information about their preservation efforts.

4. Invite students to contact one or more local environmental groups in your area (addresses can be found in the telephone book) and invite them to share data and information on their efforts to preserve the environment in your part of the country. Students may wish to ask how they and other citizens can become active in the groups' efforts.

5. Encourage students to conduct library investigations of the seashores of the United States. In which states are they located? Do they all experience the same problems as depicted in this book? What are some differing environmental concerns in various parts of the country?

6. Dr. Stephen Leatherman ("Dr. Beach") of Florida International University has ranked the best beaches in the world. Students may be interested in looking at photographs of his choices. They can do so at the Web site **http://www.petix.com/beaches/index. html**. After observing some of these choices, students may wish to post an oversize map of the world on one wall of the classroom. Encourage them to post index cards with the names of each of these beaches around the map. Yarn can be strung between each index card and the location of the designated beach on the wall map. Which state or country has the most citations?

7. Waves constantly pound the shoreline, and have done so for millions of years. As a result, sand is created through continuous wave action. Here's a fun activity that demonstrates this process:

   *Materials*: white glue, playground sand, water, small coffee can (with lid), cookie sheet

   *Directions*:

   a. Mix together six tablespoons of white glue with six tablespoons of sand in a bowl.

   b. Using the tablespoon, place small lumps of the mixture on a cookie sheet.

   c. Place the cookie sheet in a slow oven (250 degrees Fahrenheit) and bake for three to four hours.

   d. Remove the simulated rocks and allow them to cool.

   e. Put three or four rocks into a coffee can with some water and place the lid securely on top.

   f. Shake for four to five minutes and remove the lid.

   The simulated rocks will have begun to wear down; some will be worn down into sand. The action of the waves simulated inside the coffee can causes the rocks to wear against each other. As a result, they break down into smaller and smaller pieces. On a beach or shoreline, this process takes many years, but the result is the same: Rocks become smaller by being tossed against each other. Over time, rocks wear down into sand-like particles and become part of the beach or shoreline.

8. Students can build a three-dimensional model of a shoreline or tidal area with the following activity.

   *Materials*: deep baking pan (a bread loaf pan is ideal), nonstick vegetable spray, 4 cups flour, 1 cup salt, 1½ cups of warm water, acrylic or tempera paints.

   *Directions*:

   a. Knead the flour, salt, and warm water together in a large bowl for about 10 minutes (the mixture should be stiff, but pliable).

   b. Spray the baking pan with vegetable spray.

    c.   Spread the mixture into the pan, forming it into various land forms (beach, rocky shore, sand dunes, outcroppings, cliffs). If necessary, make more mixture with the same recipe.

    d.   Bake at 325 degrees for about one hour or more, depending on size and thickness.

    e.   Test the sculpture for "doneness" by sticking a toothpick into various spots (the sculpture should be firm-to-hard). If necessary, bake the sculpture longer.

    f.   Remove the sculpture from the oven and allow to cool.

    g.   Carefully slide the sculpture from the baking pan (this should be done by an adult).

    h.   Paint the sculpture with different shades of acrylic or tempera paints (available at any art, craft, or hobby store).

    i.   *Optional*: When the paint is dry, spray the sculpture with a clear varnish to preserve it.

9.   Divide the class into several small groups. Invite each group to create an environmental protection plan for the local community. Which local agencies or groups will give information? What response would students get from the local chamber of commerce or from city hall? Invite students to investigate the resources available and how those resources could be used to develop a long-range plan.

10.   Provide each of several groups of students with topographical maps of coastal states (these can be obtained through your local public library or nearby college). Invite each group to investigate the annual weather conditions for selected shores and the impact of weather on the shoreline.

11.   Invite students to create a script in which they are members of the community mentioned in the book. What would some of their responsibilities be? How would they participate in the communities' efforts to preserve their shoreline? Invite students to present answers to these questions in a brief skit or play. You may wish to assign roles and invite students to perform the skit for another class. Be sure to solicit reactions from the other class.

12.   Invite selected students to draw a series of illustrations that depict the erosion of a shoreline over several months or years. Plan time for students to discuss their illustrations and the long-term implications for the shoreline.

13.   Invite students to listen to one or more environmental music audio recordings (*Note*: An excellent collection of environmental music is produced by NorthSound, P.O. Box 1360, Minocqua, WI 54548). Afterwards, encourage students to create their own music for a seashore environment. What musical instruments (real or handmade) could be used to simulate one or more seashore sounds?

14. Invite students to discuss the advantages of people working together to preserve a part of the environment. What can a group of people do that one person cannot do? What does the phrase "strength in numbers" mean?

15. Invite students to create an ongoing newscast about a selected seashore and how wind, waves, and weather affect it over several months. Invite students to watch several television newscasts to get an idea of how they are produced. Afterwards, encourage students to create their own newscast with several reporters, eyewitnesses, and community members. Students may enjoy videotaping the newscast for later viewing.

# Chapter 8

## States and Regions

### Disappearing Lake:
### Nature's Magic in Denali National Park
Debbie S. Miller
(New York: Walker, 1997)

## Summary

This book is a wonderful tribute to the cycles of nature—particularly in Alaska. Children will understand and appreciate the wonderful interplay of plants and animals in their natural environments as a typical year unfolds in Alaska. This books offers readers perspectives of Alaska that will dispel many of the myths and misconceptions children have about our forty-ninth state.

## Social Studies Disciplines

geography

## NCSS Thematic Strands

time, continuity, and change; people, places, and environment

## Critical Thinking Questions

1. What was the most amazing thing you discovered in this book?

2. How did the illustrations contribute to your appreciation of this book?

3. What did you learn about Alaska that you didn't know before?

4. The author includes a special note at the end of the book. Why do you think she did that?

5. Which of the animals in the book would you like to learn more about?

6. How are the seasonal changes mentioned in this book similar to or different from the seasons where you live?

## Related Books

Hoyt-Goldsmith, Diane. *Arctic Hunter*. New York: Holiday House, 1992.

Levinson, Nancy. *If You Lived in the Alaska Territory*. New York: Scholastic, 1998.

McMillan, Bruce. *Salmon Summer*. New York: Walter Lorraine, 1998.

Miller, Debbie S. *A Caribou Journey*. Boston: Little, Brown, 1994.

Page, Deborah. *Orcas Around Me: My Alaskan Summer*. Morton Grove, IL: Whitman, 1997.

Thompson, Kathleen. *Alaska: Portrait of America*. Austin, TX: Steck-Vaughn, 1996.

## Activities

1. Invite youngsters to locate animal tracks in soft dirt or mud (these can be cat or dog tracks, deer tracks, or those of some other wild animal in your area). Place a circle of cardboard around the track and push it part way into the soil (be careful not to disturb the track). Mix some plaster of Paris according to the package directions. Pour it into the mold to the top of the cardboard strip. Wait until the plaster cast hardens, then remove the cast from the ground print. Remove the cardboard strip and clean the bottom. Students may wish to make several of these (for separate animals) and display them in the classroom along with pertinent research notes.

2. Students can gather delightful information and amazing facts about Alaska by logging on to the Web site **http://dac3.pfrr.alaska.edu/~ddr/ASGP/ALASKA/INDEX.HTM**. Here they will learn facts and fiction about Alaska and view scenes from around the state.

3. If students would like to see Alaska from the viewpoint of another kid, they may wish to log on to the Web site **http://tqjunior.advanced.org/3784/**. This is a site *by* kids *for* kids.

4. Divide the class into four groups. Assign each group one wall of the classroom. Invite each group to create a large, oversized mural of facts, pictures, collages, illustrations, etc. for one assigned season of the year. Each group can be responsible for adding to its mural for a designated time. Provide opportunities for students to share their murals and to tell reasons why certain objects were placed on the wall.

5. Invite students to create shoe-box dioramas of various seasonal scenes. Divide the class into several small groups. Ask each group to collect various natural objects from around the school or from their respective neighborhoods. Items can include leaves, twigs, flowers, feathers, and the like—anything that may represent part of a selected season. Invite each group to arrange their collected objects into a three-dimensional display inside a shoe box. Display the dioramas on a ledge or shelf.

6.  The National Geographic Society (Educational Services, Washington, DC 20036) produces a sound filmstrip series on the seasons. Titled *The Seasons* (catalog C03765), it describes the cycle of the seasons and seasonal changes that occur in living things. Invite students to view and review these audiovisual presentations and then prepare critical reviews for possible publication in the local newspaper.

7.  Your students may be interested in listening to traditional stories and folk tales from various cultures and countries. Contact your school librarian for suggestions. The following will get you started: *Little Sister and the Month Brothers* by Beatrice Schenk de Regniers (New York: Lothrop, Lee & Shepard, 1994); *The Old Man and His Birds* by Mirra Ginsburg (New York: Greenwillow Books, 1994); and *The Seasons and Someone* by Virginia Kroll (San Diego, CA: Harcourt Brace, 1994).

8.  Invite students to create an oversized book (a *big* book) on Alaska to include specific facts and information about the state. The book can be cut from two sheets of stiff cardboard into the shape of Alaska (staple several sheets of paper between the covers). Encourage students to contribute their book to the school library.

9. Your students may be interested in investigating the butterflies in your area of the country or in raising their own. The following products are all available from Delta Education (P.O. Box 3000, Nashua, NH 03061-3000 [1-800-442-5444]):

- Butterfly Tower (catalog 53-021-2288): Watch the growth and development of butterflies right in your own classroom. The tower includes complete instructions and a coupon for five painted lady butterfly larvae.

- Butterfly Garden (catalog 53-020-6007): This kit includes a butterfly chamber, instructions, and a coupon for butterfly larvae. It is appropriate for use indoors.

- Butterfly Feeder (catalog 53-060-3877): This feeder will attract many butterflies in the local area. Hang the feeder from a tree or mount it on a post.

10. Students may be interested in growing their own brine shrimp (similar to fairy shrimp) in the classroom. Here's a recipe along with instructions:

*Materials*:

brine shrimp eggs (brine shrimp eggs are sold as fish food for aquariums and are available from any pet store)

noniodized or kosher salt (available at most grocery stores)

2-quart pot

water

teaspoon

medicine dropper

hand lens or inexpensive microscope

aged tap water (see below)

*Directions*:

a. Fill the pot with 2 quarts of water and allow it to sit for 2 days; stir occasionally. (Most city water contains chlorine, which will kill the shrimp. Allowing it to age for several days allows the chlorine gas to escape from the water.)

b. Mix 5 teaspoons of noniodized salt with the water until dissolved.

c. Add ½ teaspoon of brine shrimp eggs to the salt water and place the pot in a warm spot.

d. Use the medicine dropper to remove some eggs from the water and observe them with a hand lens or microscope. Check a drop of water every day. Invite students to create a series of drawings or illustrations that record the growth of their brine shrimp.

e. The brine shrimp eggs will hatch in about 2 days. They will continue to grow in the water until they reach their adult stage. Students will be able to watch the shrimps' continued growth every day.

11.  Invite students to create individual or group mobiles about the state of Alaska. Invite students to record pertinent facts on the first level of each mobile. On the second level, students can hang names of tourist spots and attractions from throughout the state. On the third level, they can record names and descriptions of selected animal and plant life. Display these around the classroom.

12.  Invite students to contact the Alaska Tourism Marketing Council **http://www. travelalaska.com**. Encourage them to obtain relevant information including maps, brochures, pamphlets, and other printed materials about the state and then to create an attractive display or information center on Alaska.

13.  Invite students to write a story from the perspective of one of the animals in the story. What did that animal experience as the seasons changed? How did the animal adapt to the changing conditions? Why did the animal select its particular environmental niche? Plan time for students to share their essays.

14.  Invite students to imagine they are visiting Alaska; encourage them to write imaginary postcards to their friends and relatives and describe the sites they are visiting. Students may wish to illustrate the front of several index cards and write their messages on the back. Completed cards can be posted on a classroom bulletin board.

15.  Invite students to assemble a collage of the various state symbols for Alaska (e.g., state bird, state mammal, state fish, etc.). Students may wish to investigate the origins for some of those symbols.

# *Mailing May*

## Michael O. Tunnell

(New York: Greenwillow Books, 1997)

## Summary

When Charlotte May Pierstorff wants to cross 75 miles of Idaho mountains in 1914 to see her grandmother a problem arises: money to pay for the train ticket. With ingenuity and creativity, her parents (and the U.S. mail system) devise an ingenious plan to get her to her destination. This is a moving and beautifully told story that kids will want to hear time and again.

## Social Studies Disciplines

history, geography, economics, sociology

## NCSS Thematic Strands

time, continuity, and change; people, places, and environment; individual development and identity; production, distribution, and consumption

## Critical Thinking Questions

1. What did you enjoy most about May?

2. What are some other ways May's parents could have solved the problem?

3. How do you think May's grandmother felt when she saw May?

4. Why was travel so difficult in the early part of the twentieth century?

5. Describe the most unusual trip you have ever taken. How was it similar to or different from May's trip?

6. What would you like to include in a sequel to this book?

## Related Books

Aylesworth, Jim. *Country Crossing*. Mankato: MN: Crestwood House, 1993.

Coiley, John. *Train*. New York: Alfred A. Knopf, 1992.

Dale, Rodney. *Early Railways*. New York: Oxford University Press, 1994.

Gibbons, Gail. *The Post Office Book: Mail and How It Moves*. New York: HarperCollins, 1986.

Hynson, Colin. *Railways*. New York: Barron's Educational Series, 1998.

McNeese, Tim. *America's First Railroads*. New York: Atheneum, 1991.

## *Activities*

1. Encourage students to interview several mail carriers in your town or community. Invite students to prepare a standard list of questions to ask each carrier. When all the interviews are completed, ask students to compare the answers they gathered. Do the carriers enjoy their jobs as much as Leonard enjoys his?

2. Invite students to take a virtual tour through the San Diego Model Railroad Museum **http://www.globalinfo.com/noncomm/SDMRM/sdmrm.html** and discover first-hand information about this fascinating hobby.

3. Encourage students to log onto the Union Pacific Railroad Web site **http://www. uprr.com/uprr/ffh/history** to learn about rail travel during its early days. This site is chock-full of fascinating and descriptive information.

4. Students may wish to learn about the history of the U.S. Postal Service. Their Web site **http://www.usps.gov** offers invaluable information about this long-standing governmental agency.

5. Invite students to write a story from the perspective of a letter going through the mail system. What adventures does the letter have? What places does it visit? How long does its journey take? When stories are completed, invite a mail carrier into your classroom to discuss the actual travels of a real letter.

6. Invite students to collect postmarks from throughout the country. Encourage pupils to have their parents, friends, and relatives save envelopes from different places. These envelopes can be brought into the classroom, the postmarks can be cut from each one, and an interesting collage or display can be created on a bulletin board. Place a map of the United States next to the display and fasten yarn between each postmark and the location of that town on the map.

7. Invite a philatelist (stamp collector) into your classroom to discuss his or her hobby. What are the most unusual stamps the collector owns? What makes a stamp valuable? What are the different sizes and shapes of stamps? What are the rarest stamps in the United States? In the world?

8. If possible, take a field trip to the local post office. What are some of the jobs there? What responsibilities does the postmaster have? How many stamps are sold each day? What are some of the most unusual things postal workers have done on their jobs? Students may wish to collect answers to these and other questions and then create a poster about the postal service in their town; they can hang the poster in the post office for all to enjoy (if appropriate).

9. Students may wish to write letters of appreciation to their local postal carriers. Students may also wish to write similar letters to the postmaster in appreciation of the job he or she does every day.

10. Borrow a postal scale from the school district's business office. Bring in several packages of different weights and have students weigh them. Students may wish to create a make-believe post office, weigh several packages, chart the weights on a graph, and determine appropriate postage according to current postal rates. (These activities are a wonderful supplement to the math program.)

11. Create a contest in which students design their own original stamps. You may wish to have several different categories for the contest: funniest stamp, most original, most unusual, etc. The stamps can be judged by someone from the local post office.

12. Bring in several street maps of your local community. Talk with a mail carrier and ask that person to trace his or her daily route on the map. Discuss with students the various places the carrier visits each day, the sites he or she sees, and the different streets he or she travels. Students may want to trace their own daily routes on individual maps and compare their routes with that of the mail carrier.

13. Students may wish to create a time line of U.S. stamps. Ask students to bring in examples of U.S. stamps from 40, 30, 20, 10, and 5 years ago. Place each stamp on an index card and post it above a time line constructed over the chalkboard. Have students record significant historical events that took place when those stamps were current. Discuss reasons stamps' prices escalate.

14. Students may wish to set up a classroom post office for the class correspondence. Choose one student to be the postmaster and several to be mail carriers. All mail (papers turned in to the teacher) must be addressed (to the teacher) and have a return address (the student's name and desk location). The mail can then be placed in simulated post office boxes and inspected regularly by the classroom postmaster.

15. Divide the class into several groups. Invite each of the groups to research selected towns and cities in Idaho. Which ones would be the most difficult to connect by railroad given the geography of the land between those two cities/towns? Other students may wish to investigate rail lines between selected cities in Idaho—particularly routes that have existed since the time of this story.

16. Invite students to create a make-believe diary of a railroad postal clerk. What are the tasks he or she performs during the train ride? What sites does he or she see? Who are the people he or she encounters on the journey?

# A River Ran Wild

## Lynne Cherry

(San Diego, CA: Harcourt Brace Jovanovich, 1992)

## Summary

A beautifully illustrated book, this story concerns the "life history" of the Nashua River in New England. The stories of the people who lived along its banks, their customs, traditions, and culture and how these were shaped by the forces and resources of the river are powerfully told. The author then tells how the people polluted their river with toxins and how several residents helped return the river to its original state.

## Social Studies Disciplines

geography, sociology, political science, economics, history

## NCSS Thematic Strands

culture; time, continuity, and change; people, places, and environment; individuals, groups, and institutions; power, authority, and governance; science, technology, and society; civic ideals and practices

## Critical Thinking Questions

1. Is the Nashua River similar to any river, stream, or water source near where you live?

2. Do you believe that people intentionally set out to pollute a river? Explain.

3. How did the border illustrations (on the left-hand pages) help you learn more about the people who lived near the river?

4. As you look at the various illustrations of the river throughout the book, you will notice that the artist uses many different colors. Why do you think she did that?

5. Do you know of any other examples in which *one person* made a difference?

## Related Books

Fredericks, Anthony D. *Simple Nature Experiments with Everyday Materials.* New York: Sterling, 1995.

Hoff, Mary. *Our Endangered Planet: Groundwater.* Minneapolis, MN: Lerner, 1991.

————. *Our Endangered Planet: Rivers and Lakes.* Minneapolis, MN: Lerner, 1991.

Javna, John. *50 Simple Things Kids Can Do to Save the Earth.* Kansas City, MO: Andrews and McMeel, 1990.

Stille, Darlene. *Water Pollution.* Chicago: Children's Press, 1990.

## *Activities*

1. Invite students to contact various community agencies and county groups on environmental preservation efforts in your local area. What is being done by local groups, organizations, and governmental bodies to preserve and protect the local environment? What laws, rules, or regulations are in effect? How are those laws enforced? What forms of punishment are in effect?

2. Encourage students to invite several county commissioners or members of the town council to your classroom to discuss environmental preservation issues in their jurisdictions. Students may wish to ask how the needs of the community are balanced against the needs of local businesses and industries.

3. Invite children to visit a nearby stream or river. Encourage them to look carefully at the water as it flows by. Invite them to dip an empty plastic container into the water and raise it to their noses to smell. Ask them to sniff the air. Ask them if they noticed any of the following:

   - *A smell of rotten eggs.* Streams with this odor are heavily polluted with dumped sewage.

   - *A shiny or multicolored film on the surface.* Oil or gasoline have been dumped into these streams.

   - *A noticeably green tint to the water.* These waterways probably have a lot of algae growing in them. Too much algae means there isn't enough oxygen in the water for fish and plant life.

   - *Foams or suds floating in the water.* This usually means that detergents or other soapy wastes are leaking into the water from nearby factories and/or homes.

   - *Cloudy or extremely muddy water.* This indicates mud, dirt, or silt in the water. It also means that plants and animals may not be getting enough oxygen. Another cause may be soil erosion upstream.

   - *Bright colors, such as orange or red, on the surface.* This is usually a sign that pollutants are being released into the stream by factories or industries upstream.

Inform children that clean, clear, and transparent water that has no smell is the best kind of water for aquatic plants, animals, and humans.

If a polluted water source is detected in your area, invite youngsters to select one or more of the following actions to raise public consciousness about the polluted waterway:

a.    Invite them to write a letter to the editor of the local newspaper.

b.    Create a series of posters or signs to post with local businesses.

c.    Prepare a brief public service announcement (a local advertising agency can assist you with this) for distribution to local radio stations.

d.    Write a letter of complaint to a local or state legislator informing that individual of the polluted waterway.

e.    Ask the local newspaper to insert a flyer or leaflet in an edition of the daily paper.

f.    Create an inexpensive leaflet and ask that it be placed in the grocery bags of patrons at the local supermarket.

g.    Have students send a letter of concern to the local chamber of commerce.

Encourage youngsters to brainstorm for additional activities and outreach efforts. What other ways can they think of that will inform the public and inspire people to do something about a polluted or endangered waterway?

4. Invite students to visit a local garden center or nursery and obtain information on plants and trees that are indigenous to your part of the country. Request funds from the local PTA or PTO to purchase plants that can be planted in and around the school (secure the principal's permission first). Plan time for students to discuss the civic responsibilities of all community members in beautifying and/or cleaning up their particular neighborhoods.

5. Invite students to question neighbors in their community about how they work to preserve and protect the plants and animals in the local area. Invite students to gather their findings into various charts and graphs to be displayed in the classroom.

6. Invite students to write to the following organizations and request information and data on river and stream protection:

> The Isaak Walton League of America
> 1401 Wilson Blvd., Level B
> Arlington, VA 22209

Invite kids to request a copy of their free *Save Our Streams* booklet as well as other information.

> Renew America
> 1400 16th St., Suite 710
> Washington, DC 20036

Renew America has a collection of environmental success stories—stories about kids who have made a difference.

> 20-20 Vision
> 69 South Pleasant St., #203
> Amherst, MA 01002

20-20 Vision can locate the address of any government official in the country—great if kids want to send their letters to specific bureaucrats.

> Keep America Beautiful
> 99 Park Ave.
> New York, NY 10016

This group prepares a brochure titled *Pollution Pointers for Elementary Students*— a list of environmental improvement activities.

7. Encourage students to establish a litter patrol for your school. They may wish to establish a recruiting station to solicit volunteers for their teams, place posters in and around the school, establish regular patrols throughout the school grounds, and create a flyer or newsletter about the cleanup to be sent to administrators.

8.  The following Web sites offers youngsters loads of fascinating information about the environment and about their roles in protecting and preserving it.

> **http://tqjunior.advanced.org/3715/**
>
> **http://eelink.net/sitemap.html**
>
> **http://solstice.crest.org/environment.eol/toc.html**
>
> **http://www.cais.com/publish/**
>
> **http://www.niehs.nih.gov/kids/kids.htm**
>
> **http://takeaction.worldwildlife.org**

9.  The following experiment will help youngsters learn about various forms of pollution and its effects on the environment. (*Note:* This activity requires adult supervision and guidance.)

*Materials*: Provide children with four empty, clean baby food jars. Label the jars "A," "B," "C," and "D."

*Directions*: Fill each jar halfway with aged tap water (regular tap water that has been left to stand in an open container for 72 hours). Put a half-inch layer of pond soil into each jar, add one teaspoon of plant fertilizer, then fill each jar the rest of the way with pond water and algae. Allow the jars to sit in a sunny location or on a window sill for two weeks.

Next, work with the youngsters to treat each jar as follows:

   Jar A: add two tablespoons of liquid detergent

   Jar B: add enough used motor oil to cover the surface

   Jar C: add half a cup of vinegar

   Jar D: do not add anything

Allow the jars to sit for four more weeks.

Children will notice that the addition of the motor oil, vinegar, and detergent prevents the healthy growth of organisms that took place during the first two weeks of the experiment. Those jars now show little or no growth happening, yet the organisms in jar D continue to grow.

Detergent, motor oil, and vinegar are pollutants that prevent organisms from obtaining the nutrients they need to continue growing:

- The detergent illustrates what happens when large quantities of soap are released into a waterway.

- The motor oil demonstrates what happens to organisms after an oil spill.

- The vinegar shows what can happen to organisms when high levels of acids are added to a pond or stream.

Children will be able to see the effects of various pollutants on their miniature ecosystems. Plan time to discuss the implications of large quantities of these pollutants discharged into a waterway over a long time. What would be the short-term and long-term consequences of such actions? Plan adequate time to discuss these issues; provide opportunities for youngsters to describe their feelings in a journal or to make them known through various public relations efforts (see above).

10. Invite students to create a time line for the story. They may wish to post a large sheet of newsprint on one wall of the classroom or to use a long strip of adding machine tape. Encourage small groups of students to record significant events in the story on appropriate places on the paper. Students may elect to record other significant historical events (as part of a larger historical unit) throughout the school year.

11. Invite children to look at the border illustrations on the left-hand pages. Each of those drawings is related to the period described in the accompanying text about the river. Provide opportunities for students to investigate (through various library resources) the border drawings and their relationships to the time frame of the story on that page. On one page, for example, the author talks about the "start of the new century" and the various things that were happening on the Nashua River. The border illustrations on that page include the first telephone, an Edison phonograph, the first bicycle, the first camera, and the first sewing machine. Invite youngsters to research the reasons those items were important to that time. Why did the artist/author select those particular items? What others, not included, *could* be included on this page? What items are more representative of that time?

# *Welcome to the Sea of Sand*

## Jane Yolen

(New York: G. P. Putnam's Sons, 1996)

## Summary

A lyrical and beautifully illustrated paean to desert life, this book provides young readers with an intriguing and interesting look at a most misunderstood ecosystem. The plants and animals that inhabit this environment are richly presented and graphically detailed in vibrant language and mesmerizing drawings. This is a wonderful book to read aloud to any class.

## Social Studies Disciplines

geography

## NCSS Thematic Strands

people, places, and environment

## Critical Thinking Questions

1.  What was the most unusual plant or animal in the book?

2.  Would you enjoy living in this ecosystem?

3.  What surprised you the most about desert life?

4.  What might be some environmental concerns regarding the desert?

5.  This book tells about the Sonoran desert. How is it similar to or different from other deserts?

6.  Why are deserts important?

## Related Books

Arnold, Caroline. *A Walk in the Desert.* Englewood Cliffs, NJ: Silver Press, 1990.

Baker, Lucy. *Life in the Deserts.* New York: Watts, 1990.

Hogan, Paula. *Expanding Deserts.* Milwaukee, WI: Gareth Stevens, 1991.

Siebert, Diane. *Mojave.* New York: HarperCollins, 1998.

Silver, Donald. *One Small Square: Cactus Desert.* New York: W. H. Freeman, 1995.

Twist, Clint. *Deserts.* New York: Dillon Press, 1991.

Wallace, Marianne. *America's Deserts.* Golden, CO: Fulcrum, 1996.

## *Activities*

1. Students may enjoy creating their own desert terrarium. The following instructions will help them design a fully functioning terrarium:

    a. Fill the bottom of a large glass container with a layer of coarse sand or gravel. Combine one part fine sand with two parts of potting soil and spread this over the first layer.

    b. Sprinkle lightly with water.

    c. Place several varieties of cactus into the terrarium (it might be a good idea to wear gloves). Most nurseries carry cacti or they can be ordered through the mail from selected seed companies and mail-order nursery houses.

    d. When planting the cacti, be sure that the roots are covered completely with the sandy mixture.

    e. You and your students may decide to place several desert animals (such as lizards or horned toads) in the terrarium. As above, be sure the animals have enough food and water available.

    f. The desert terrarium can be left in the sun and does not need a glass cover. It should, however, be lightly sprinkled with water about once a week.

2. Students may enjoy creating their own desert dictionary. Invite them to form small groups—with each group responsible for gathering words and definitions for several letters of the alphabet. For example:

    a. Atacama Desert

      Australian Thorny Devil

      Ananuca Lily

    b. Beetles

      Blue Gilia

    c. Camel

      California Poppy

    d. Desertification

    e. Endangered Environment

    f. Frilled Lizard

      Fennec Fox

    Students may wish to contribute their class dictionary to the school library.

3. Invite students to write to one or more of the following national parks and request information about the flora and fauna. When the brochures, flyers, leaflets, and descriptive information arrives, invite students to assemble it into an attractive display in the classroom or in a school display case.

Death Valley National Park
P.O. Box 579
Death Valley, CA 92328

Joshua Tree National Park
74485 National Park Dr.
Twentynine Palms, CA 92277

Great Basin National Park
Baker, NV 89311

Big Bend National Park
Big Bend, TX 79834

4.  Students may wish to visit a local gardening center or nursery. Invite them to purchase a cactus (these are typically inexpensive). Invite them to observe their cacti carefully—what shape are they? Does the shape change as the plant grows? What do the needles look like? Students may wish to observe cactus features with a magnifying lens and record their observations in a desert journal.

5.  Divide your class into several small groups. Encourage each group to practice reading one or more pages. Invite the groups to record the entire book on audiotape (several practices may be necessary). Students may wish to suggest several sound effects (e.g., slithering snakes, swooping hawks, etc.), too. Invite students to contribute the tape to the school library.

6.  Students can stay up-to-date on the latest events, discoveries, and news about life in the deserts of the United States by accessing the Web site of *Desert USA Magazine*—**http://www.desertusa.com**. Here they can learn about the lives of the flora and fauna that inhabit deserts in the United States. They may wish to gather selected information together in the form of descriptive brochures or pamphlets for the classroom library.

7.  Students may wish to take a virtual tour of a desert at **http://www. mobot.org/mbgnet/sets/desert/ index.htm**. Here they will learn what a desert is like, what causes deserts, deserts of the world, desert plants and animals, and desert life at night. This is a wonderful site chock-full of information.

8. Deserts are often described as areas in which less than 10 inches of rain falls each year. Invite students to compare the amount of rain that falls in their part of the country with the amount of rain that falls in parts of the Sonoran Desert (approximately from one to three inches per year). The following activity will help them to measure rainfall accurately in their area.

   This instrument helps students accumulate rainfall data over an extended period—a week, a month, a year.

   *Materials*: a tall jar (an olive jar works best), a ruler, a felt-tip pen, a funnel

   *Directions*:

   a. Use a ruler and a felt-tip pen to mark off quarter-inch intervals on the side of the olive jar.
   b. Place a funnel in the jar and leave it outside in a secure location. (The funnel will help collect the rainwater as well as help prevent evaporation from taking place.)
   c. Invite students to use a chart or graph to record the amount of rain your area gets in a week or a month (see table 8.1).
   d. Students may wish to compare their findings with those reported in the local newspaper.

**Table 8.1. Rainfall Data**

| My Town/City | The Desert |
|---|---|
| One Day _____ | _____ |
| One Week _____ | _____ |
| One Month _____ | _____ |
| One Year _____ | _____ |

9. Invite students to create salt-map deserts. Provide them with the following recipe and encourage them to work in teams to create an original depiction of the Sonoran Desert.

   *Materials*: 1½ cups of coarse salt (kosher salt works well), 1 cup of flour, 1½ cups of water.

   *Directions*: Invite students to mix the salt and flour together in a medium-size mixing bowl. Add enough water to make a stiff dough. Students should form the mixture on a piece of stiff cardboard or small sheet of plywood (invite them to work quickly). Invite students to shape their mixture into hills, mountains, large flat areas, or other geographical features that represent the Sonoran Desert. Allow the mixture to dry for about two to three days. When the mixture is dry, students can paint it with tempera paints.

10. Students may wish to make their own sand drawings. Obtain packages of colored sand from a local craft or hobby store. Provide each student with a square of stiff cardboard and a bottle of school glue. Encourage students to create an illustration of a desert scene by using the glue as though it were a paintbrush. Before the glue dries, students should sprinkle small amounts of colored sand onto the glue to create interesting mosaics or motifs. Allow the paintings to dry for several days and display them in the classroom.

11. Invite students to grow several different varieties of cactus in the classroom. Cacti can be obtained very inexpensively from most nurseries and garden supply shops. Encourage students to investigate the conditions necessary for their cacti to thrive in a classroom. How are those conditions similar to or different from the conditions in the Sonoran Desert?

12. Invite students to note and record the different types of animal noises they hear in and around their homes. Are there animals that make noises only in the morning or only at night? How do the animals in your students' part of the country compare with the animals (and the noises they make) in the desert? Students may wish to make Venn diagrams of the similarities and differences.

13. Divide the class into several groups and invite each group to plan a trip across the desert. Encourage each group to assemble a list of supplies and equipment they would need for the journey. What items would be essential? What might they expect to see? Invite students to compare their information and then compile lists to be posted on the bulletin board for class discussions.

# Chapter 9

## Nation and Country

### Flood!
**Mary Calhoun**
(New York: Morrow Junior Books, 1997)

## Summary

This is a fictionalized account of one family's struggles during the disastrous Midwestern floods of 1993. It tells of the human tragedy, heartache, and misery that accompanied that natural disaster. But, it also celebrates the human spirit and the determination and tenacity of people working together for a common cause. This is a timeless tale to be shared with listeners of any generation.

## Social Studies Disciplines

geography, history, economics, sociology

## NCSS Thematic Strands

time, continuity, and change; people, places, and environment; individual development and identity; individuals, groups, and institutions; civic ideals and practices

## Critical Thinking Questions

1. What did you admire most about Sarajean?

2. Is Sarajean's grandmother similar to anyone in your family or to any of your friends?

3. What would you find to be the scariest part of a flood?

4. Why do you think the family felt so strongly about staying in the house?

5. What do you think happened to the house at the end of the story?

6. What would you like to say (if you could) to Sarajean at the end of the story?

## *Related Books*

Badt, Karin. *The Mississippi Flood of 1993*. New York: Children's Press, 1997.

Hiscock, Bruce. *The Big Rivers: The Missouri, the Mississippi, and the Ohio.* New York: Atheneum, 1997.

Lauber, Patricia. *Flood: Wrestling with the Mississippi*. Washington, DC: National Geographic Society, 1996.

Sipiera, Paul, and Diane Sipiera. *Floods*. New York: Children's Press, 1998.

Waterlow, Julia. *Flood*. New York: Thomson Learning, 1993.

Waters, John. *Flood!* Mankato, MN: Crestwood House, 1991.

## *Activities*

1. Invite students to log on to the PBS Web site **http://www.pbs.org/newshour/infocus/floods.html**.to track current information about floods. Here they will learn the *hows* and *whys* of floods, flood fighters, pet rescues, and see real floods on video. This is a super site with loads of fascinating information.

2. Another Web site maintained by PBS, **http://www.pbs.org/wgbh/nova/flood/**, provides students (and their teachers) with up-to-the-minute information about current floods around the country in addition to lesson plans and classroom resources. Contact them and obtain some of this amazing information for your students.

3. Invite your students to compose an essay on what they would take with them should a flood approach their houses. Suggest that they can take only those items they can carry in their arms on one trip. What is most important to them? What do they value most? Plan time to discuss students' responses.

4. Invite a local meteorologist or weather forecaster from the local television station of a college to visit your class. Suggest that the weatherperson share information on the causes of floods and why they are so prevalent in certain areas of the country.

5. Contact the local chapter of the American Red Cross and invite a representative to address your class on the efforts of this organization during a natural disaster such as a major flood. What are their responsibilities? How can the average citizen become involved in the efforts of the Red Cross during a flood in another part of the country? Students may wish to assemble information into a classroom brochure or notebook.

6. Invite each student to write about a memorable storm he or she has experienced. What made that storm so unforgettable? What was the scariest part about that storm? How did they prepare for the storm? Encourage students to share their experiences as a class.

7. Invite students to look through several old magazines and prepare collages of some of the materials (e.g., wheelbarrows, shovels, ladders, etc.) that the people in the book might have used in their fight against the rising waters. Post the collages on a classroom bulletin board.

8. Encourage students to measure and calculate the amount of water it would take to fill your classroom up to the five-foot level (for example). They will need to calculate the dimensions of the room (in cubic feet) and determine the amount of water (in gallons) of one cubit foot and multiply.

9. The book doesn't quite end. Invite your students each to write a sequel to the story. What happened to the family? What happened to the house? Plan time to discuss the various endings.

10. Invite students to make a list of all the different ways in which water is used in their homes (cooking, drinking, bathing, etc.). How many different ways is water used around the house? Encourage students to compute the average amount of water used in the home each day. Students whose families use city water may be able to use their monthly water bill to compute a daily average.

11. Students may wish to create their own well. Invite them to obtain a large aluminum can (a coffee can works well). A cardboard tube (from a roll of paper towels) can be placed upright in the can. Pour a layer of gravel inside the can around the outside of the tube. Pour another equal layer of sand on top of the gravel. Pour in water until it reaches the top of the layer of sand. Invite students to notice what happens inside the tube. Explain to them that this is the same process used for obtaining well water.

12. Invite students to obtain several different water samples from in and around their homes (e.g., tap water, water from a standing puddle, rainwater, etc.). Encourage them to place a coffee filter over each of several glass jars. Then, invite students to pour each of the water samples into a separate jar. Encourage students to note the impurities that have been trapped by each of the filters. Which type of water has the most impurities?

13. Invite students to gather newspaper and/or magazine articles about weather or bring in information from daily weather forecasts that are contained in local newspapers or television news shows. Articles can be filed in shoe boxes and shared in a weather news area. Encourage students to examine all the clippings and compile a list comparing and contrasting the different types of forecasts.

14. Invite students to talk about rain and how it makes them feel. They may wish to complete the following sentence stems orally or in writing:

    Rain tastes like _____

    Rain smells like _____

    Rain looks like _____

    Rain sounds like _____

    Rain feels like _____

15. The following activity allows youngsters to see what a raindrop looks like:

    Invite children to fill a cake pan (9-x-15 inches) with about two inches of sifted all-purpose flour. At the start of a rainstorm, encourage kids to stand outside for a few moments and collect approximately from 30 to 50 raindrops in the flour (This will have to be done quickly and at the beginning of a rainstorm. Just a few moments in the rain will be sufficient). Have them bring their pans inside and allow them to sit overnight.

    The next day, encourage children to sift gently through the flour and gather up all the congealed raindrops they can. Have them organize the drops on a flat surface (the kitchen counter). They will note that raindrops come in two basic sizes—large and small (large raindrops fall from higher clouds and thus gather more moisture than small rain drops). Children will also note that the drops will be in a state of expansion or contraction. (As a drop falls, it expands and contracts—a natural atomic reaction. Depending on when it hits the pan of flour, it will have either expanded or contracted.)

    Children may wish to preserve their raindrops. They can do this by spraying the drops with a commercial varnish (or by carefully dipping them in the varnish). When the drops are dry, youngsters will be able to manipulate them in a variety of activities.

16. Invite students to check an almanac for the yearly rainfall for your area. Then, they can locate several cities in the United States and find the normal annual precipitation. Encourage them to compare the rainfall in several cities with that of your town or city. They can then plot the information on a large chart. Invite students to note any similarities or differences.

17.  Students may enjoy observing and recording the weather patterns that occur in your area of the country. Be sure that students have an opportunity to record weather conditions over a long period (from two to three months, if possible). You may wish to create your own weather notebook so that students can keep track of rainfall, cloud conditions, temperature, humidity, barometric pressure and the like. A Weather Watching Kit (catalog 5J-738-2253) is available from Delta Education, P.O. Box 950, Hudson, NH 03051. Also available from the same company are two classroom weather charts—*Chalkboard Weather Station* (catalog 57-230-1639) and *Weather Chart* (catalog 57-230-1640).

18.  Obtain a copy of *USA Today*. Show students the color weather map on the back of the first section. Invite them to note the various designations used to record weather information. Encourage students to read through the weather section and to note the predictions for your area. Invite students to create a special weather map similar to the *USA Today* map, but tailored for your geographic region (as opposed to the entire United States).

# Home: A Journey Through America

## Thomas Locker

(San Diego, CA: Harcourt Brace, 1998)

## Summary

From the seacoasts to the plains to the desert, this collection of poems and prose defines what America is to many of us. The author, a talented illustrator, has captured the sentimentality and beauty of the American experience in a delightful collection of insights from some of our most talented writers—from Abraham Lincoln to Willa Cather. In so many ways, this book is a celebration of the voices and spirit of America. This is a wonderful accompaniment to any study of the United States.

## Social Studies Disciplines

geography, sociology, history

## NCSS Thematic Strands

time, continuity, and change; people, places, and environment; individuals, groups, and institutions; civic ideals and practices

## Critical Thinking Questions

1. Which of the literary pieces did you enjoy the most? In what ways did it affect you?

2. How did the illustrations contribute to your appreciation of this book?

3. Was there a home left out of the book? What type of home would you like to add?

4. Which of the scenes was most similar to where you live?

5. Is there something in this book you would enjoy sharing with members of your family? If so, what is it?

## Related Books

Brenner, Martha. *Abe Lincoln's Hat*. New York: Random Library, 1994.

Delafosse, Claude. *Landscapes*. New York: Cartwheel Books, 1996.

Fisher, Leonard. *The Oregon Trail*. New York: Holiday House, 1990.

Greene, Carol. *Caring for Our Land*. New York: Enslow, 1991.

Hall, Donald. *Ox-Cart Man*. New York: Viking, 1979.

King, Penny. *Landscapes*. New York: Crabtree, 1996.

Miller, Jay. *American Indian Families*. New York: Children's Press, 1997.

Pelta, Kathy. *Eastern Trails: From Footpaths to Turnpikes*. Austin, TX: Steck-Vaughn, 1997.

Sanders, Scott. *Aurora Means Dawn*. New York: Bradbury Press, 1989.

## *Activities*

1. A popular recipe in many parts of this country is shortcake. This recipe has been around since colonial times and has been served in homes across the country throughout our country's history. You and your students may enjoy making this delicious (and historical) treat:

> ### SHORTCAKE
>
> ✓ 2 cups of flour
> ✓ 1½ teaspoons of baking powder
> ✓ ½ teaspoon salt
> ✓ 2 tablespoons of shortening
> ✓ ¾ cup of milk
> ✓ 3 tablespoons of sugar
>
> Combine the dry ingredients (with the exception of one table-spoon of sugar) in a medium-sized mixing bowl. Slowly cut in the shortening and then add the milk. Grease an eight-inch-square baking pan with shortening. Pour in the dough and distribute it evenly throughout the pan. Sprinkle the surface with one table-spoon of sugar. Bake at 375 degrees for 20 minutes. Allow to cool and cut into squares. Enjoy!

2. Invite each student to write a short poem about his or her home, community, or neighborhood. What are some of the special features and characteristics that should be celebrated in each poem?

3. There are no cities celebrated in this book. Invite students to form themselves into small groups. Invite each group to choose a city in the United States and develop a piece of prose or poetry for that urban area. Invite groups to post their creations on a classroom bulletin board.

4. Invite students to write letters to students in another class as though your students were traveling across the country. Encourage each student to describe the adventures he or she encountered on the journey from west coast to east coast. Encourage students from the other class to respond to those letters.

5. Students may wish to consult such books as *The Old Farmer's Almanac Book of Weather Lore* by Edward F. Dolan (New York: Yankee Books, 1988); *Questions and Answers About Weather* by M. Jean Craig (New York: Four Winds Press, 1969); or *Weather* by Paul E. Lehr (New York: Golden Press, 1965). Encourage students to create a series of weather maps for the different sections of the United States mentioned in the book. Students may wish to obtain additional information about regional weather patterns via the following Web sites:

   **http://www.princeton.edu/Webweather/ww.html**

   **http://www.weatheronline.com**

   **http://www.wunderground.com**

   **http://www.accuweather.com/weatherf/index_corp**

6. Invite students to create a travel guide for each of the regions referred to in the book. Students may wish to obtain a collection of maps and travel guides for selected states from a local travel agent. Encourage students to put together an itinerary for anyone wishing to duplicate the imaginary journey referred to in the book.

7. Provide small groups of students each with a large quantity of Popsicle sticks (available at any hobby or variety store) and some white glue. Invite each group to construct a complete house (walls, roof, windows, door, etc.) without using any drawings or plans. When this is completed, encourage students to discuss the difficulties they had. Plan time to discuss the differences between a house and a home. The class may want to talk about why the author titled the book as he did.

8. Students will enjoy seeing the filmstrip series titled *The Westward Movement* (No. 04102, National Geographic Society, 1979). This two-part series describes the forces that influenced westward expansion and the men and women who made it happen. Although this series is geared for an older audience (from grades 5 to12), younger students will find it an appropriate introduction to pioneer life, particularly if lots of classroom discussion follows.

9. Songs and singing have always been an important part of life in the United States. You can choose from numerous collections to introduce your students to the ballads and folk songs that were and still are a part of our heritage. Here are some songbooks to get you started: *Woody Guthrie Folk Songs: A Collection of Songs by America's Foremost Balladeer* (Ludlow Music, Inc.); *Wake Up and Sing: Folk Songs from America's Grassroots* by Beatrice Landeck and Elizabeth Crook; and *American Folk Songs for Children* by Ruth Crawford Seeger (Doubleday).

10. Share a recent copy of *USA Today* with your class. Invite students to create their own national newspaper by selecting each of the regions mentioned in the book and developing one or more newspaper articles pertinent to each selected area. Students may wish to focus on the people of each region, its culture, sports teams, climate, or other selected topics. Two or three students in each group can be responsible for gathering relevant facts about their region and contributing articles for the class newspaper.

11. Invite students to select one or more famous Americans from each of the regions illustrated in the book. Invite students to consult library resources and present a compendium of biographical information to the class. This data can be assembled into a large classroom notebook or onto a special bulletin board display.

12. Encourage each student to put together a minibook about the various places he or she has lived during his or her life. Each child can contribute a poem or piece of prose related to each area and accompany each one with an original illustration. All the minibooks can be gathered into a large notebook.

13. Invite students to collect several copies of travel magazines and brochures and then prepare a collage of pictures clipped from those periodicals. Students may wish to create collages depicting the same areas of the country portrayed in the book. Plan time to discuss their creations with the class.

14. Invite students to make an audio recording of the book. Students may select and include appropriate musical selections for background music and then add sound effects. Students may wish to share their recording with another class.

15. When traveling across the country, one needs to eat. Here's a fun-to-make and fun-to-eat treat that travelers have been munching for years—granola. Provide your students with an opportunity to create this wholesome snack.

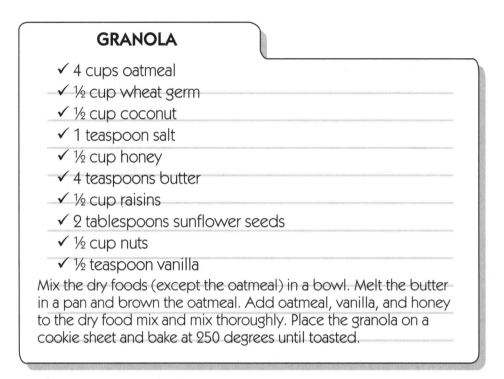

**GRANOLA**

- ✓ 4 cups oatmeal
- ✓ ½ cup wheat germ
- ✓ ½ cup coconut
- ✓ 1 teaspoon salt
- ✓ ½ cup honey
- ✓ 4 teaspoons butter
- ✓ ½ cup raisins
- ✓ 2 tablespoons sunflower seeds
- ✓ ½ cup nuts
- ✓ ½ teaspoon vanilla

Mix the dry foods (except the oatmeal) in a bowl. Melt the butter in a pan and brown the oatmeal. Add oatmeal, vanilla, and honey to the dry food mix and mix thoroughly. Place the granola on a cookie sheet and bake at 250 degrees until toasted.

16.  Our country has a national flag and each state has its own state flag. Invite students to select appropriate books and reference materials from the library and challenge them to design and develop selected regional flags. For example, what might be an appropriate regional flag for each region illustrated in the book? Which features from those regions should be included on each flag? What should each flag say about the history or particular characteristics of that region?

17.  Students can learn more about various geographical regions of the United States by accessing one or more of the following Web sites.

**http://www.odci.gov/cia/publications/factbook/us.html**

**http://www.lib.utexas.edu/Libs/PCL/Mapcollection/
      unitedstates.html**

**http://pittsford.monroe.edu/Schools/Jefferson/Maps&Globes/
      MapsGlobesFrame.html**

**http://www.ipl.org/youth/stateknow/**

# *The Rough-Face Girl*
## Rafe Martin
### (New York: G. P. Putnam's Sons, 1992)

## Summary

A scarred face does not prevent the rough-face girl from seeing the beauty of the earth around her, nor does it disguise her beautiful, kind heart in this award-winning retelling of a powerful Algonquin Cinderella. This is a book to share again and again.

## Social Studies Disciplines

anthropology, sociology, history

## NCSS Thematic Strands

culture; time, continuity, and change; people, places, and environment; individual development and identity

## Critical Thinking Questions

1. How is this story similar to *Cinderella*?

2. What did you admire most about the rough-face girl?

3. Who do you think the Invisible Being is?

4. Does this story remind you of any events in your own life?

5. How did the illustrations help you appreciate or understand the story?

6. What would you like to say to the two older daughters?

## Related Books

Climo, Shirley. *The Egyptian Cinderella*. New York: HarperCollins, 1992.
———. *The Korean Cinderella*. New York: HarperTrophy, 1996.
Louie, Ai-Ling. *Yeh-Shen: A Cinderella Story from China*. New York: Paper Star, 1996.
Perkal, Stephanie. *Midnight: A Cinderella Alphabet*. New York: Shen's Books, 1997.
Pollack, Penny. *The Turkey Girl: A Zuni Cinderella*. Boston: Little, Brown, 1996.
San Souci, Robert. *Sootface: An Ojibwa Cinderella Story*. New York: Bantam Books, 1997.
Schroeder, Alan. *Smoky Mountain Rose: An Appalachian Cinderella*. New York: Dial Books for Young Readers, 1997.

*Note*: More than 50 different children's books—all revolving around the *Cinderella* theme—can be found in an extensive bibliography listed at **http://www.acs.ucalgary.ca/~dkbrown/ cinderella.html**.

## *Activities*

1.  Invite students to create puppets for the story by decorating old socks with markers, colored paper, bits of yarn, or other scraps. Divide the class into small groups and assign one scene of the story to each group. Invite each group to paint a background for its scene on butcher paper or an old bedsheet. Hang the background on a bulletin board or use a table turned on its side for the puppet theater.

2.  You may wish to provide your students with old bedsheets and fabric scraps. Using the book as a guide, encourage students to create costumes like the ones worn by the characters in the story. Students may wish to dramatize their favorite parts of the story.

3.  The stars were an important part of Native American stories and culture. Your students may enjoy investigating the role of stars and constellations through Native American Astronomy's delightful and informative Web site **http://indy4.fdl.cc.mn.us/~isk/stars/ starmenu.html**.

    As a follow-up, invite students to create informative brochures or leaflets on the roles of stars and constellations for various Native American cultures.

4.  Here are three other Web sites that will provide your students with important and significant information about selected Native American tribes:

    **http://www.germantown.k12.il.us/html/intro.html**

    **http://www.si.edu/nmai/**

    **http://www2.scsn.net/users/pgowder/dancing.htm**

5.  Students may wish to investigate specific information about the Algonquin Indians. The following Web site, **http://dickshovel.netgate.net/alg.html** is devoted exclusively to the Algonquins, their customs, their traditions, and their lifestyle (*Note*: The author of the site has used the more traditional spelling of *Algonkin*).

6.  The Algonquin Indians were located primarily along the upper Ottawa River in Canada. Invite students to calculate the distance from their town or city to this part of North America. Hang a large world map on the wall and invite students to plot a travel route to this part of the world. What means of transportation could be used? How long would the trip take?

7.  The Algonquin Indians were primarily hunters. Invite your students to investigate various library resources to determine some of the indigenous animals the Algonquin may have hunted. Invite students to assemble a guide to the native animals of that region of North America.

8.  The Algonquin Indians did engage in some marginal farming—primarily raising corn. Corn is a staple in many American Indian diets as it is in ours. Invite students to make parched corn from the following American Indian recipe:

> **PARCHED CORN**
> ✓ 3 tablespoons butter
> ✓ 3 cups dried corn
> ✓ salt
>
> Melt the butter in a large frying pan. Put one layer of corn kernels into the pan and heat over a medium-high heat, stirring constantly. The kernels will be done when they turn brown and puff up (approximately four minutes). Add salt to taste and serve.
>
> (*Note*: Students may be interested in learning that more than 65 percent of our contemporary diet can be traced directly to the contributions of Native Americans.)

9.  Plan to share some of the *Cinderella* stories from other cultures with your students (see above). Invite students to note the similarities and/or subtle differences between the versions. What elements are present in all versions? What modifications and/or adaptations have been made in selected versions? Invite students to construct an over-sized wall chart that illustrates the plots (and details) of various *Cinderella* stories in colorful detail.

10. Invite students to create a sequel to the story that focuses on the life of the rough-face girl and the Invisible Being. How did they spend their lives after they were married? Where did they live? Did they have children? If so, what kind of adventures did they have?

11.   The following Web sites offer teachers a variety of teaching ideas using various versions of *Cinderella* from around the world (e.g., *Tattercoats, Cap o' Rushes, The Twelve Months,* and *The Princess and the Golden Shoes*). Access these sites and share these wonderful projects with your students.

**http://www.acs.ucalgary.ca/~dkbrown/tatter.html**

**http://www.acs.ucalgary.ca/~dkbrown/caprush.html**

**http://www.acs.ucalgary.ca/~dkbrown/twelve.html**

**http://www.acs.ucalgary.ca/~dkbrown/princess-gold.html**

12.   According to some estimates, there are more than 300 versions of the *Cinderella* story from around the world. The following is a humorous readers theatre adaptation of *Cinderella*. Invite your students to produce this version and discuss any similarities and/or differences between this adaptation and the version or versions with which they are more familiar.

# Cinderella Visits the Shoe Store and Gets a Pair of Air Jordans

## Staging

The narrator should be standing to the side of the two major characters. Cinderella and the shoe salesman can be seated on tall stools or chairs (see figure 9.1).

|  | Cinderella X | Shoe Salesman X |
|---|---|---|
| Narrator X | | |

**Fig. 9.1. Staging for** *Cinderella Visits the Shoe Store and Gets a Pair of Air Jordans.*

**Narrator:** Once upon a long time ago there was this semiprincess—you know, the kind of princess who lived in this big ugly castle with her big ugly stepsisters and her big ugly stepmother. Every day she would wash and wax all the floors in this big ugly castle while her big ugly stepsisters and big ugly stepmother would go to all the dances and parties throughout the kingdom (of course, nobody ever danced with these big ugly women simply because they were just *too* big and *too* ugly . . . but they went to all the parties anyway). Of course, since Cindy (as she was known to her friends) did so much washing and waxing of the floors, she would often run out of floor soap and floor wax and would have to visit her local supermarket to buy more. Well, this one day, while she was walking around the local mall, she happened to pass by a shoe store. She was looking in the window at all the shoes when she got this brilliant idea. So she went in.

**Cindy:** (*excited*) Hey, Mr. Shoe Salesman! Do you happen to have any shoes that I could wear to the next ball at the local palace. You see, I'm hoping some tall, dark, and handsome prince will come along, sweep me off my feet, put me in his magic carriage, and carry me off to his enchanted castle in the next kingdom . . . or something like that.

**Salesman:** Hey, hold your horses. You obviously don't know your fairy tales very well. Don't you know you've got to have some fairy godmother come along first and give you the finest dress in all the land and create a pumpkin with tiny horses to drive you to the local palace.

**Cindy:** (*forcefully*) Look, get real! This is the new age. I'm going to get myself some of the latest fashions from Europe and really knock out all those princes hangin' around the castle tonight. I'll be so good lookin' that every prince in the place will want to dance with me. All I need is the right pair of shoes and I'll be the hit of the ball.

**Salesman:** Look, the object of the story is not to have the best looking pair of shoes, but rather to have a pair of shoes that don't fit too well so that when you're running down the castle steps at the stroke of midnight, one of the shoes will fall off and be found by one of those tall, dark, and handsome princes, who will race around the city the next day to try it on all the young ladies, except that you're the only one who can fit into the shoe, so you're the one who gets to marry the lucky prince.

**Cindy:** (*excited*) Listen, Jack! That may be your version of the story, but it's not mine. See, in my version of the story I'm the one in charge. I get to choose which prince I want to dance with and if he's no good, then I'll just drop him like a ton of bricks. Frankly, I'm tired of playing second fiddle to all these guys in all these fairy tales who get most of the action and most of the good lines. You know, now that I think about it, I think it's high time we fairy tale women get equal billing in these stories. It's about time we get the major roles, the major movie contracts, and the major bucks for doing these stories. For too long we've been taking it on the chin, storywise . . . and now we're going to stand up for our rights. (*more excited*) Yeah, yeah, yeah! In fact, let's forget about those fancy-dancy Italian pumps, those fancy-dancy parties at the castles, and those fancy-dancy princes with their noses stuck so far up in the air that they're getting nosebleeds. I'm changing my mind. After all, this is *my* story. You know what I'd really like to have, instead of some stupid dancing shoes, is a pair of Air Jordans. (*forcefully*) And while I'm thinking of it why don't we just forget about this whole palace ball and prince thing too. What I'd really like to do is take on a few of those hotshot princes in a game of one-on-one. Let's see if those fancy-dancy princes can shoot some three-pointers and make a couple of slam dunks. Yea, they haven't seen nothin' yet.

**Salesman:** Well, if you say so. If you'll wait just a moment I'll get a few pairs of Air Jordans from the back.

**Narrator:** And so it was that Cinderella totally forgot about the palace ball and the stupid princes who had nothing better to do with their time than run around the village testing some high heel slippers on some of the smelliest and stinkiest feet in the whole county. Meanwhile, Cindy was off organizing her own summer basketball league with a couple of the characters from other fairy tales. Cindy, along with Little Red Riding Hood, Rapunzel, Sleeping Beauty, and Snow White eventually formed their own basketball team and whipped the socks off of every team that challenged them that summer. Later, Cindy was approached by representatives of a major shoe manufacturer to create her own brand of sneakers. She eventually retired a very rich woman.

Reprinted from Anthony D. Fredericks, *Frantic Frogs and Other Frankly Fractured Folktales for Readers Theatre* (Englewood, CO: Teacher Ideas Press, 1993).

# The Seasons Sewn

## Ann Whitford Paul

### (San Diego, CA: Browndeer Press, 1996)

## Summary

This is a book about quilting, about the seasons of the year, and about life in early America. Beautifully told and wonderfully illustrated, it shares the magic of design and the American creative spirit with young and old alike. Full of information about pioneer life and the trials and tribulations of the time, the book is also a celebration of family and community. You and your students will be turning to this book again and again—it is a delight!

## Social Studies Disciplines

geography, sociology, economics, history, anthropology, political science

## NCSS Thematic Strands

culture; times, continuity, and change; people, places, and environment; individual development and identity; individuals, groups, and institutions; production, distribution, and consumption; civic ideals and practices

## Critical Thinking Questions

1. Which of the quilts in this book did you enjoy the most?

2. What aspect of pioneer life appealed to you the most?

3. What kinds of trials or tribulations would you experience if you had lived 200 years ago?

4. Why are some of the quilt designs so intricate, yet others are relatively simple?

5. What is the most amazing piece of information you learned from this book?

## Related Books

Benner, Cheryl. *The Boy and the Quilt.* New York: Good Books, 1991.
Howard, Ellen. *The Log Cabin Quilt.* New York: Holiday House, 1997.
Jonas, Ann. *The Quilt.* New York: Puffin Books, 1994.
Kinsey-Warnock, Natalie. *The Canada Geese Quilt.* New York: Yearling, 1992.
Lyons, Mary. *Stitching Stars: The Story Quilts of Harriet Powers.* New York: Aladdin, 1997.
Paul, Ann. *Eight Hands Round: A Patchwork Alphabet.* New York: HarperCollins, 1996.
Willard, Nancy. *The Mountains of Quilt.* New York: Voyager, 1997.

## *Activities*

1.  Invite students to create a large collage on quilting or sewing. Encourage them to cut out pictures and illustrations from old magazines and paste them onto a large sheet of paper. Examples of clothing, sewing materials, dyes, sewing machines, etc. can all be included on the collage. Invite students to prepare an explanatory sheet of the finished product.

2.  Students may enjoy making simple looms. Provide each student with a 6-x-8-inch piece of scrap wood. Along each six-inch end, hammer six nails evenly spaced. Encourage students to use string or twine and wrap tightly between the nails (these vertical threads are called the *warp*). Then have students use colorful yarn, ribbon, or fabric strips to weave over and under the warp threads (the horizontal threads are called the *woof*). Encourage students to tighten each row with a comb or fork, then tie off the loose ends or tuck them into the fabric. The finished products can be displayed throughout the room.

3.  If possible, bring in a handmade quilt and a machine-made quilt. Invite students to examine the two quilts for similarities and differences. Ask students to assume the roles of quality inspectors to decide which quilt has the better construction.

4.  Check with a local women's club or the telephone book to locate a sewing or quilting organization. Invite several members of the group to demonstrate their craft to students. Provide an opportunity for students to interview club members on the intricacies of quilt making.

5. Invite each student bring in a piece of fabric from an outgrown item of clothing. Create a classroom quilt by using tacky glue and attaching the fabric squares to cardboard. Students may also wish to work in small groups and stitch the squares into strips, and then combine them to form a large quilt-top. They can then sew the quilt-top to a plain blanket and hang it on one wall of the classroom.

6. Encourage students to interview their grandparents or other older people about their recollections of quilts or quilting. Students may wish to compare and share the results of their interviews with each other.

7. Invite students to compose essays on how their lives are different from the lives of the children depicted in the book. Encourage youngsters to illustrate their stories (they may wish to emulate the style of Currier and Ives, which is used in the book).

8. Encourage students to each design and develop a quilt (or a quilting square) that tells of an important event in their lives. Plan opportunities for students to share their quilts with each other.

9. Most quilts made during the late 1700s and early 1800s were dyed with natural dyes (unlike the artificial dyes used for fabrics today). Invite your students to prepare one or more of the following dyes and test them out on swatches of white fabric (cotton strips, for example). Afterwards, invite them to discuss any differences between natural and man-made dyes.

    *Cranberry Dye*:

    Combine two cups of cranberries and one quart of water in a stainless steel pot and simmer for 15 minutes. Remove pot from the stove, crush the berries, and then simmer for an additional 15 minutes. Strain the mixture through a sieve; discard the berries. Add the cotton swatch to the warm mixture for 30 minutes or more, remove, and allow to dry.

    *Walnut Shell Dye*:

    Combine two cups of walnut shells and one quart of water in a stainless steel pot and leave to soak overnight. Boil for at least one hour, then strain the mixture through a sieve; discard walnut shells. Add a cotton swatch to the warm mixture. Remove the swatch after 30 minutes.

    *Mustard Dye*:

    Mix ½ cup of prepared mustard with one quart of water. Heat to boiling. Remove pot from the stove and place a swatch of cotton in the mixture for 30 to 60 minutes.

10. Invite students to look for animal tracks around the school grounds. Encourage them to photograph the tracks. When the photos have been developed, invite students to work in small groups to create a specialized quilt pattern for a designated series of tracks. Students may wish to conduct additional investigations in the library to gather information about each of their quilted animals.

11. Invite students to create a time capsule of selected events in their lives. What occurrences, celebrations, or events would each student like to include in her or his time capsule? Invite each student to create a collection of illustrations or photographs that would be "sealed" until opened by another child in the future (in 100 years, for example). What mementos should students include in their time capsules?

12. Students may wish to create a time line that illustrates the events and historical stories as depicted in the book. Encourage students to contribute personal descriptions and original drawings.

13. Invite small groups of students to design and assemble separate books titled *Family Holidays*, *Community Holidays*, *Regional Holidays*, *Statewide Holidays*, and *National Holidays*. Students may wish to conduct library investigations and create descriptive handbooks or brochures on specific types of holidays celebrated throughout the country or just within their own area.

14. People in the 1700s and 1800s raised and prepared their own food. Today, most of our food comes from a supermarket. In fact, most students have not eaten home-prepared foods. Following is a recipe from colonial times for home-baked bread that your students may enjoy preparing (and certainly eating):

### EARLY AMERICAN BREAD

- ✓ 3–3 $\frac{1}{2}$ cups all-purpose flour
- ✓ 1 package active dry yeast
- ✓ $\frac{1}{3}$ cup packed brown sugar
- ✓ 1 teaspoon salt
- ✓ 3 tablespoons shortening or butter
- ✓ 2 cups whole wheat flour

Combine 2 cups all-purpose flour and yeast. Heat and stir brown sugar, shortening, 1$\frac{3}{4}$ cups water, and 1 teaspoon salt until warm. Add to flour mixture and beat for three minutes at high speed. Stir in whole wheat flour and as much remaining all-purpose flour as you can. Knead until moderately stiff. Shape into a ball, place in a lightly greased bowl, and let rise in a warm place for one to two hours. Punch dough down and let rest for 10 minutes. Separate into two equal parts and place each into a lightly greased loaf pan. Bake at 375 degrees for 40 to 45 minutes. Remove from pans, slice, spread with butter or homemade jam, and enjoy!

# When Jessie Came Across the Sea

**Amy Hest**

(Cambridge, MA: Candlewick Press, 1997)

## Summary

This is a touching and delightful story about hope, desire, and eternal love. Young Jessie is chosen by the village's rabbi to journey to America—a land where the streets are paved with gold: a land of plenty. She makes the arduous trip, begins work in her cousin's shop, and learns to read English. After being reunited with her beloved grandmother, she experiences the "American Dream." This is a definite read-aloud book—one that all generations can share and treasure.

## Social Studies Disciplines

geography, sociology, political science, economics, history

## NCSS Thematic Strands

culture; time, continuity, and change; people, places, and environment; individual development and identity; individuals, groups, and institutions; power, authority, and governance; global connections

## Critical Thinking Questions

1. What did you admire most about Jessie?

2. Would you be willing to make a trip similar to Jessie's?

3. Did Jessie's experiences in America match her dreams?

4. What are some acts of bravery that you have accomplished in your life?

5. How would you describe this story to your friends?

6. What is the most memorable event from the book?

## Related Books

Bratman, Fred. *Becoming a Citizen: Adopting a New Home.* Austin, TX: Steck-Vaughn, 1993.

Jacobs, William. *Ellis Island: New Hope in a New Land.* New York: Atheneum, 1990.

Kroll, Steven. *Ellis Island: Doorway to Freedom.* New York: Holiday House, 1995.

Levine, Ellen. *If Your Name Was Changed at Ellis Island.* New York: Scholastic, 1994.

Quiri, Patricia. *Ellis Island.* New York: Children's Press, 1998.

Reef, Catherine. *Ellis Island*. New York: Dillon Press, 1991.

Ryan, Susannah. *Coming to America: The Story of Immigration*. New York: Scholastic, 1996.

Stein, Richard. *Ellis Island*. New York: Children's Press, 1994.

## *Activities*

1.  Invite students to each take on the role of Jessie. Encourage them to write daily letters back to the grandmother while they are aboard the ship. What should they include in those letters? What information would they like to share daily with their "grandmothers"? Invite students to gather their letters in a large classroom notebook and then share them at regular intervals.

2.  Students may be interested in learning more about Ellis Island, its history, and the thousands of people who came to this country through this national landmark. The following Web sites can provide your students with relevant information:

    **http://www.icgnet.com/users/phil/ruins/ellis/index.html**

    **http://www.neco.org**

    **http://www.ellisisland.org**

3. Students may wish to log on to the National Immigration Forum's Web site **http://www.immigrationforum.org**. Here they can learn about the reunification of families, the rescue of refugees, and the equal treatment of immigrants under the law.

4. Encourage students to create an oath in which they agree to read with their parents for at least 15 minutes each day. Students may wish to design a contract (that you and they will sign) vowing to support the oath.

5. Provide students with modeling clay and ask each one to create a bust of a favorite family member. Discuss the reasons for their choices. When the busts are completed, set up a gallery for them in the classroom.

6. Students may be interested in creating a family time line. Have them ask their parents about the marriage dates, birth dates, and deaths of various family members. Invite students to record these dates on index cards for a time line to be displayed on one wall of the classroom. (Attach lengths of string across one wall of the room and use clothespins to clip the index cards to the string in the correct order.)

7. Invite students to create a large class scrapbook of the activities they enjoy with their grandparents. The scrapbook could include photographs with accompanying captions as well as illustrations of holidays or family gatherings.

8. Encourage students to conduct interviews with the oldest members of their families. They can conduct the interviews in person, by telephone, or by mail. Invite students to ask about the most memorable events in their relatives' lives and about the reading materials their relatives may have used when they were children. Provide opportunities for students to share their discoveries in writing or orally.

9. Students may enjoy creating a family newspaper. Assign students the roles of reporters and ask them to interview family members about their opinions of current events, about their hobbies, their free-time activities, and their vacation spots, for example. Students can assemble the information on each family into a sheet of news and then collect the sheets into a large family newspaper.

10. Invite students to gather data on the literacy rates of various countries around the world. Which countries have the highest literacy rates? Invite them to discuss the reasons the United States does not have the highest literacy rate of all of the industrialized countries.

11. Invite students to bring in photographs of family members. Encourage students to use pushpins to indicate family members' countries of origin on a large world map. Post the pictures next to the countries of origin.

12. Invite a member of the local literacy or reading council to visit your classroom to discuss illiteracy. Encourage your students to ask questions about the extent of the problem and about what is being done to solve it.

13. Invite students to create special charts or graphs of literacy activities in your classroom. For example, number of books read over a certain time (e.g., one month); number of hours spent reading at home; number of hours spent reading versus number of hours spent watching television; and/or number of books checked out of the school library during a marking period. Students may wish to compare their figures with those of another class.

14. Schedule a family read-in. Invite parents, grandparents, and other adults to visit the classroom at a scheduled time (during the school day, immediately after school, or in the evening). Direct each person to bring a collection of his or her favorite books and a pillow or two. Schedule a block of time (e.g., one hour) for everyone to gather in a central location and read silently. Afterwards, participants may wish to share some of their thoughts or the things learned via their reading.

15. Invite students to write a sequel to the story. What happens to Jessie in 5, 10, or 20 years? What adventures or life experiences does she have? Does she ever return to her homeland? Do she and her husband have children? What does she tell the children about her journey or about her grandmother?

16. Invite students to calculate the distances from various European countries to the United States. Students may wish to pin lengths of yarn to a wall map of the world indicating the various distances. Encourage students to investigate the forms of transportation immigrants from selected countries may have used from the time they departed their homes or towns until they arrived at Ellis Island.

17. Invite students to conduct library investigations on the immigration rates from various countries. For example, how many immigrants traveled from northern Europe during the last part of the nineteenth century? How many immigrants came from southern Europe during the early part of the twentieth century? How many immigrants came from Japan in the 1930s?

18. If possible, contact your local city hall and arrange to invite several recent immigrants to this country to come and share their experiences with your class. You may wish to invite one or two who have recently become U.S. citizens. Students may wish to ask the immigrants why they came to this country, why they decided to become U.S. citizens, and how the United States is different from their countries of origin.

19. The illustrations in this book are incredible; invite each student to select her or his favorite. Encourage each youngster to share the reasons for his or her choice. How does that illustration reflect the tone or theme of the book? Invite students to write a fictitious letter to the artist inviting him to illustrate a single event in their lives. What specific event would each student choose as the most important, significant, or memorable for Mr. Lynch to illustrate? Plan time for students to discuss their choices.

20. Students may be interested in reading other books illustrated by P. J. Lynch. The following would make wonderful additions to any classroom library: *The Christmas Miracle of Jonathan Toomey* by Susan Wojciechowski (Cambridge, MA: Candlewick Press, 1995); *Catkin* by Antonia Barber (Cambridge, MA: Candlewick Press, 1996); and *The King of Ireland's Son* by Brendan Behan (New York: Orchard, 1997).

# Chapter 10

*World*

## Elephants for Kids
**Anthony D. Fredericks**
(Minnetonka, MN: NorthWord Press, 1999)

## Summary

Filled with awe-inspiring details, this book gives readers incredible facts and information about the world's largest land animal. The narrator (a native of Kenya) offers readers insights to this often misunderstood animal. The book provides a wonderful bridge between social studies and science.

## Social Studies Disciplines

geography

## NCSS Thematic Strands

people, places, and environment; global connections

## Critical Thinking Questions

1. What was the most amazing thing you learned from this book?

2. How is the narrator's life similar to yours?

3. What do you think should be done to preserve the dwindling populations of elephants around the world?

4. Is the behavior of elephants similar to that of any other animal?

5. What makes an elephant such a fascinating animal?

6. What would you like to share with the author of this book?

## Related Books

Arnold, Caroline. *Elephant*. New York: Morrow Junior Books, 1993.

———. *Kenya (Postcards From)*. Austin, TX: Raintree, 1996.

Kagda, Falaq. *Kenya (Festivals of the World)*. New York: Gareth Stevens, 1997.

Patent, Dorothy Hinshaw. *African Elephants: Giants of the Land*. New York: Holiday House, 1991.

Pringle, Laurence. *Elephant Woman*. New York: Atheneum, 1997.

Sammis, Fran. *Colors of Kenya*. Minneapolis, MN: Carolrhoda, 1998.

Smith, Roland. *African Elephants*. Minneapolis, MN: Lerner, 1995.

Weiss, Ellen. *The African Elephant*. New York: Workman, 1996.

## Activities

1. The National Geographic Society (**http://www.nationalgeographic.com**) has a variety of videos that offer an intriguing look into the richness and vastness of the African continent. Try to obtain one or more of the following: *Africa's Animal Oasis* (No. 51529); *Africa* (No. 51440); *Journey to the Forgotten River* (No. 51461); *Serengeti Diary* (No. 51388); *African Odyssey* (No. 51336); *Bushmen of the Kalahari* (No. 51027); *African Wildlife* (No. 50509); *Africa's Stolen River* (No. 51373); and *Lions of the African Night* (No. 51331).

2. Students gather information about Kenya through **http://www.globalfriends. com/html/world_tour/kenya/kenya.htm**. Here, they will discover information about the land and its people, language and expression, daily life, celebrations, and creative arts. Students may wish to assemble selected data into a descriptive brochure or notebook.

3.  Students can download a complete map of Kenya from **http://www.pathfinder. com/travel/maps/images/KENYA.GIF**.

4.  Students will love to access **http://www.supersurf.com/kenya/**, which was created by a 12-year-old boy in Phoenix, Arizona. Here, they will find lots of information about this fascinating country.

5.  Classes in many parts of Kenya are typically held outdoors. If possible, conduct a day's worth of lessons on the school grounds. Afterwards, invite students to reflect on the differences experienced between outdoor education and indoor education. How would they feel about having all their classes outdoors? What difficulties would they encounter? What modifications in the current program would have to be made?

6.  Peanut soup is a popular dish in many parts of Kenya. Here's a recipe you and your students may enjoy preparing and sharing:

## PEANUT SOUP

✓ 2 celery sticks, 2 carrots, 2 onions, 2 potatoes, 2 tomatoes
✓ 4 cups water
✓ 2 bouillon cubes (any flavor)
✓ 2 teaspoons salt
✓ 1 teaspoon pepper
✓ 1 cup chunky peanut butter
✓ 1 cup milk
✓ 2 tablespoons brown sugar
✓ 6 tablespoons rice

Cut the vegetables into small pieces and place in a large saucepan. Add the water, bouillon cubes, salt, and pepper and boil gently for about 20 minutes, stirring occasionally. Blend the peanut butter, milk, and brown sugar in a mixing bowl and add to the saucepan. Stir in the rice; simmer for about 30 minutes. Ladle into bowls and enjoy!

7.  Students may enjoy creating a book of elephant facts. Invite them to obtain several books and resources from the school or public library (see above) on elephants and their habits. The information can be collected into a book constructed in the shape of an elephant (bind two pieces of cardboard and several sheets of paper; cut into large elephant shapes).

8. Elephants are threatened and endangered. Children can learn more about elephants and other endangered animals throughout the world by obtaining copies of or subscribing to one or more of the following children's magazines:

> *Audubon Adventure*
> National Audubon Society
> 613 Riversville Rd.
> Greenwich, CT 06830

> *Chickadee*
> Young Naturalist Foundation
> P.O. Box 11314
> Des Moines, IA 50340

> *Dolphin Log*
> Cousteau Society
> 8430 Santa Monica Blvd.
> Los Angeles, CA 90069

> *Naturescope*
> National Wildlife Federation
> 1912 16th St., NW
> Washington, DC 20036

> *Ranger Rick*
> National Wildlife Federation
> 1412 16th St., NW
> Washington, DC 20036

> *Zoobooks*
> Wildlife Education, Ltd.
> 930 West Washington St.
> San Diego, CA 92103

9. Invite children to write to one or more of the following environmental agencies to obtain relevant literature on endangered species around the world. When the material arrives, invite children to make a list of those animals that are most seriously imperiled, those that are endangered, and those that are threatened.

> National Wildlife Federation
> 8925 Leesburg Pike
> Vienna, VA 22184

> National Audubon Society
> 666 Pennsylvania Ave., SE
> Washington, DC 20003

Friends of Wildlife Conservation
New York Zoological Society
185 St., Southern Blvd.
Bronx Zoo
Bronx, NY 10460

10. Encourage students to adopt an endangered animal. Write to the American Association of Zoological Parks and Aquariums (4550 Montgomery Ave., Suite 940N, Bethesda, MD 20814) and ask about their animal adoption program. For a few dollars, kids will be assigned an endangered animal and receive a photograph and fact sheet about their adoptee. The money sent is used to care for and feed selected endangered animals.

11. Invite students to present a minilesson to another class on Kenya or elephants. The lesson can be presented in person or via a videotape.

12. Invite a zoologist or biologist from a local college to visit your classroom and share information related to elephants. Invite students to prepare questions beforehand to be sent to the guest speaker.

13. Read the poem "African Dance" by Langston Hughes aloud to the class (this poem can be found in many poetry anthologies). Read it again and invite students to keep a steady beat with the rhythm of the poem by beating homemade drums, clapping hands, or using special rhythm instruments.

# The Ever-Living Tree

**Linda Vieira**

(New York: Walker, 1994)

## Summary

Readers will be able to watch the world unfold as a tiny sequoia begins its life in a foggy forest. Marco Polo reaches China, Columbus launches his ships, the Mayflower lands in the New World, and the United States declares its independence—all the while, the tree continues to grow. Eventually it becomes one of the tallest living things on Earth. Its history and the history of civilization are inexorably intertwined in this beautifully illustrated book; you will refer to it time and again.

## Social Studies Disciplines

geography, anthropology, sociology, political science, history, economics

## NCSS Thematic Strands

culture; time, continuity, and change; people, places, and environment; individuals, groups, and institutions; power, authority, and governance; production, distribution, and consumption; science, technology, and society; global connections; civic ideals and practices

## Critical Thinking Questions

1. Why do you think the author decided to tell the history of the world through the life of a single tree?

2. How did the illustrations contribute to your understanding of the historical events?

3. What was the most important piece of information you learned about the tree?

4. Which of the historical events mentioned in the book would you like to learn more about?

5. Why are trees important?

## Related Books

Baron, Kathy. *The Tree of Time: A Story of a Special Sequoia*. San Francisco, CA: Yosemite Association, 1994.

Bosveld, Jane. *While a Tree Was Growing*. New York: Workman, 1997.

Collard, Sneed. *Green Giants*. Minnetonka, MN: NorthWord Press, 1994.

Dowden, D. D. *The Tree Giants: The Story of the Redwoods, the World's Largest Trees.* New York: Falcon, 1988.

Hiscock, Bruce. *The Big Tree.* New York: Atheneum, 1991.

Markle, Sandra. *Outside and Inside Trees.* New York: Bradbury, 1993.

Reed-Jones, Carol. *The Tree in the Ancient Forest.* Nevada City, CA: Dawn Publications, 1995.

Thornhill, Jan. *A Tree in a Forest.* New York: Simon & Schuster, 1992.

Wadsworth, Ginger. *Giant Sequoia Trees.* Minneapolis, MN: Lerner, 1995.

## *Activities*

1.  A number of organizations and groups provide free (or minimally priced) brochures and other information on trees to the public. Invite youngsters to write to one or more of the following groups and ask for pertinent literature:

    Forest Service
    U.S. Department of Agriculture
    P.O. Box 96090
    Washington, DC 20090
    (Ask for the poster *How a Tree Grows.*)

    U.S. Geological Survey
    P.O. Box 25286
    Denver, CO 80225
    (Ask for *Tree Rings: Timekeepers of the Past.*)

    American Forestry Association
    Global ReLeaf
    P.O. Box 2000
    Washington, DC 20013

    National Arbor Day Foundation
    100 Arbor Ave.
    Nebraska City, NE 68410

2.  The following organizations and groups offer loads of information and important data on how to plant and grow trees. Invite youngsters to request relevant brochures and documents.

    TreePeople
    12601 Mulholland Dr.
    Beverly Hills, CA 90210

Worldwatch Institute
1776 Massachusetts Ave., NW
Washington, DC 20036

American Forestry Association
Global ReLeaf
P.O. Box 2000
Washington, DC 20013

National Arbor Day Foundation
100 Arbor Ave.
Nebraska City, NE 68410

When material from these groups arrives, invite youngsters to organize it into various categories. These could include one or more of the following: *Growing Tips, Forests and Forestry, Saving Our Forests, Growing a Tree, North American Trees, How to Care for a New Tree,* and *Trees and Our Future.*

3.  Invite youngsters to plant a tree in their yards, in a local park or playground, or alongside a nearby road. Visit a local nursery or gardening center. Consult the staff about what kind of tree to plant. Talk with students about the factors that will help them select the most appropriate tree(s). These may include initial cost, care and maintenance, location, climate, availability of nutrients, soil conditions, long-term needs, aesthetic value, and whether or not the tree is native to the local area.

    Follow appropriate planting instructions for the tree (the staff of the gardening center or nursery can help you with this, too). Invite students to start a journal on the life of the tree in its new location. They can record its height, diameter, width, condition, number of leaves, number of branches, and other pertinent data. Encourage them to keep a running record of the tree for several months, a year, or several years.

4.  Invite children to gather information and data from the school and/or public library. They can put together a booklet or notebook titled *Tree Olympics*—a compendium of the world records held by individual trees, varieties of trees, or groups of trees throughout the world. Finding the following world records may help get them started:

    World's tallest tree
    World's oldest tree
    World's smallest tree
    World's widest tree
    Tree with the longest roots
    Tree with the biggest seeds
    Tree with the smallest seeds
    Tree with the widest leaves
    Most common tree
    Rarest tree

The information can be researched and recorded in a journal or notebook for sharing with others.

5. Trees for Life (1103 Jefferson, Wichita, KS 67203) is an organization that uses its profits to plant fruit trees in underdeveloped countries. For a fee of $.50 per student, the organization will send you seeds, individual cartons for planting, and a teacher's notebook. The type of tree they send will depend on the state in which you live; they send only trees that are native to your region. Students will enjoy watching their seeds sprout and (eventually) grow into trees.

6. Invite each student to select a tree on the school grounds and to adopt that tree for the length of the school year. Students can take photographs of their trees, make bark rubbings, and observe and record animal and plant life in and around the trees. Encourage students to observe their adoptees regularly (once a week, for example) and to maintain individual journals of their observations, predictions, experiments, etc. throughout the school year. If trees are very young, students may wish to create baby albums for them.

7. Discuss the importance of recycling newspapers as a significant way of saving trees. Explain that approximately every four-foot stack of newspapers equals the wood from one tree. Designate one corner of your room or hallway as a newspaper recycling center. Invite students to begin saving newspapers and stacking them in the designated area. Once a week, measure the stack of newspapers, record the measurement on a chart, and place a figure of a tree on the chart for each four feet of newspapers.

8. Invite students to write to the National Arbor Day Foundation (100 Arbor Ave., Nebraska City, NE 68410) and request a copy of *The Conservation Trees* brochure. This brochure explains how trees help the environment. Invite students to draft a similar document that would apply to the trees in your area.

9. Invite an employee of a local garden center or nursery to visit the classroom and discuss the trees that are native to your area. What planting techniques should be used? How should trees be cared for? Why are some trees easier to grow than others? Invite students to gather the responses to those questions (as well as their own) into an informative brochure or leaflet that could be distributed at the garden center or nursery.

10. Invite students to create a time line of the historical events mentioned in the story. They may wish to use some of the examples along the top of each page as models for their own time line. Post a long strip of adding machine tape along one wall of the classroom and record and illustrate individual or collective historical events in their appropriate positions.

11. Invite students to record their own growth throughout the school year. Students can post separate sheets of newsprint on a wall of the classroom. Invite each student to record her or his height along one edge and significant events in the life of the classroom along the other edge. Invite students to compare their charts with the events recorded in the book.

12. Divide the class into several small groups. Invite each group to choose one of the historical events in the book and then develop it into an appropriate shoe-box diorama. Provide groups with the necessary supplies (yarn, construction paper, paints, chalk, scissors, etc.) and encourage them to create three-dimensional representations of the chosen event inside a shoe box. Provide an appropriate display for these dioramas.

13. In the lower right corner of each two-page spread in the book are illustrations of various artifacts, dwellings, or items related to the historical event being described in the text. Invite students to create their own versions of some of these objects using the following recipe for simple clay:

### SIMPLE CLAY

- ✓ 3 cups baking soda
- ✓ 1½ cups cornstarch
- ✓ 2 cups warm water

Pour the baking soda and cornstarch into a medium sized pot. Add the warm water and mix thoroughly. Heat at a medium heat until the mixture boils. Stir constantly. Remove pot from the stove and allow to cool. Add some food coloring (if desired) and knead the clay. It can now be shaped into various forms and allowed to dry. Store in a closed container (the clay will dry quickly when left exposed).

14. Your students may enjoy viewing photographs of Northern California and other areas where redwood trees grow. The following Web site **http://www.travelmedia.com/connected/redgal.html** can provide them with wonderful photos of this region.

# *Great Crystal Bear*
## Carolyn Lesser
### (San Diego, CA: Harcourt Brace, 1996)

## *Summary*

This lyrical and poetically engaging book blends fact and fiction into a delightful and mystical tale about a single polar bear and his journey through a year. This is an incredible book that will open the reader's eyes and ears to the magic of language and the enchantment of a tale well told.

## *Social Studies Disciplines*

geography

## *NCSS Thematic Strands*

people, places, and environment; global connections

## *Critical Thinking Questions*

1.  How was this description of a single animal similar to or different from other animal books you have read?

2.  How did the illustrations help you learn more about this magnificent creature?

3.  What was the most amazing fact you learned about polar bears?

4.  How are polar bears different from other bears?

5.  What would you like to share with the author of this book?

## *Related Books*

Brimner, Larry. *Animals That Hibernate*. New York: Watts, 1991.

Chinery, Michael. *Questions and Answers About Polar Animals*. New York: Kingfisher, 1994.

Fair, Jeff. *Bears for Kids*. Minocqua, WI: NorthWord Press, 1991.

Gill, Shelley. *Alaska's Three Bears*. New York: Paws IV, 1990.

Penny, Malcolm. *Bears*. New York: Bookwright, 1990.

Petty, Kate. *Bears*. New York: Gloucester Press, 1991.

Sackett, Elisabeth. *Danger on the Arctic Ice*. Boston: Little, Brown, 1991.

## *Activities*

1. Provide students with opportunities to blend a poetic phrase with a factual detail, two poetic phrases, or two factual details to create a unique combination. This process (known as *word addition*) can be illustrated with the following example.

   swirls of snow on the ice
   + waving curtains of light
   ———————————————
   the vast Arctic night

   In the example above, the phrase *swirls of snow on the ice* was added to the phrase *waving curtains of light* to create the *the vast Arctic night*. Here are two more examples.

   swans take flight
   + daylight hours are shorter
   ———————————————
   fall is coming

   retreating sea ice
   snow geese huddled on nests
   + the sun rises higher
   ———————————————
   spring arrives

   Invite youngsters to choose some of their favorite phrases from the book and use them to create their own word addition problems. Youngsters may wish to begin by adding two phrases together and progress to the addition of three or four phrases to create unique addends.

2. The National Geographic Society (P.O. Box 96580, Washington, DC 20077-9964 [1-800-343-6610]) produces several wonderful videos, including *Polar Bear Alert* (catalog 51290); *Giant Bears of Kodiak Island* (catalog 51654); *The Grizzlies* (catalog 51300); and *Secrets of the Wild Panda* (catalog 51997). If possible, obtain one or more videos and show them to students. Discuss with students any differences between the events shown in the videos and those described in the books above. How accurate were the videos in depicting the life of a specific bear? What information was left out? What information should have been included?

3. Invite students to write to the Office of Endangered Species, U.S. Fish and Wildlife Service, Department of the Interior, Washington, DC 20240 to obtain information on the current status of endangered species of bears. When the information arrives, invite students to create special posters to inform the public about the status of specific species.

4. Invite students to create a series of bar graphs illustrating the life span of different species of bears. Which species has the longest life span? Which the shortest? Does a bear's life span change when it is confined at a zoo or wildlife animal park? Students may wish to contact a zoologist or biologist at a nearby college to obtain answers.

5. Invite students to form small groups and research bear legends and tales from different countries or cultures. Students may wish to duplicate stories and gather them into a bound book (e.g., *Bear Legends of Native Americans*). Some students may wish to examine various bear constellations (e.g., *Ursa Major*) and report their findings to the class.

6. Invite students to examine and explore a variety of Arctic life through the following Web site: **http://www.arcticexplorer.com/english/arclife.htm**. Encourage them to assemble their information in the form of brochures and/or pamphlets for display in the school library.

7. Invite students to create a time line for the story and record it on a strip of adding machine tape or on a large sheet of newsprint. Encourage students to add illustrations of events from the story as well as any other additional information learned through books and/or Web site information (see above). Invite students to discuss the annual events of the polar bear's life and how those events might relate to the annual events in their own lives.

8. Invite students to assume the roles of newspaper reporters. Encourage them to write newspaper articles that chronicle the various events in a polar bear's life as well as the changes that occur in an Arctic environment. Students may wish to create a newspaper organized around selected sections (*sports*—how far a polar bear walks in a day; *front page*—a killing on the ice; *weather*—seasonal changes in temperature; *business*—the economic impact of killing too many seals).

9. Invite students to create an ongoing trivia game, each student contributing from 5 to 10 questions and answers. They can play the game regularly (as they accumulate more information about this ecosystem) or as a "final exam" at the conclusion of the unit.

10. Focus on a different environment each day (e.g., Monday—the Arctic; Tuesday—the rainforest; Wednesday—the desert; and so forth). Each day include stories, songs, student-created plays, trivia, games, and environmental concerns related to the specific ecosystems. Invite a speaker from a local environmental group or college to discuss current issues related to a specific worldwide environment.

11. Invite students to create a word poem about life in the Arctic. Write the name of an Arctic animal, event, celebration, or environmental feature vertically on the left side of a piece of poster board. Encourage students to suggest words or phrases that are indicative of that item for each letter in the designated word. Following is an example for the Arctic:

> **A**lways cold
>
> **R**ainbows of color
>
> **C**logged with ice
>
> **T**ime sometimes stands still
>
> **I**nuits hunt for food
>
> **C**aptivating scenery

12. Invite a travel agent to visit your classroom. Ask him or her to discuss various trips or excursions available to the Arctic. Invite the agent to work with your students in planning an imaginary trip for the class to take to and across the Arctic.

13. Invite students to create an imaginary diary as it might be written by the polar bear in the story. What thoughts might the bear have in its journey? What are some of its reactions to various events and circumstances? What are some memorable incidents in its life? Encourage students to work in small teams and to share their entries.

14. Invite students to create a salt map of the Arctic regions of the world. Share a globe or two-dimensional map with them and encourage them to create their own representations using the following recipe:

## SALT MAP

✓ 2 cups salt

✓ 1 cup flour

✓ 1½ cups water

Mix the salt and flour together in a medium-sized mixing bowl. Add just enough water to make a stiff dough. Lay the mixture on a piece of stiff cardboard or thin board and shape into the desired shapes. Allow to dry (approximately one to two days) and paint with tempera paints. (*Note:* This recipe will produce a salt map that will last for a long time.)

# *How to Make an Apple Pie and See the World*

## Marjorie Priceman
### (New York: Alfred A. Knopf, 1994)

## Summary

Making an apple pie is really very easy . . . unless, of course, the market is closed. This delightful story takes the reader on a trip throughout various countries to obtain the necessary ingredients for a perfect apple pie. Full of whimsy and delightful illustrations, it will spark lots of magical discussions and delicious memories.

## Social Studies Disciplines

economics, geography, sociology

## NCSS Thematic Strands

people, places, and environment; production, distribution, and consumption; global connections

## Critical Thinking Questions

1.  Did this book make you hungry?

2.  What was the most unusual country visited in this book?

3.  What was the most unusual ingredient included in the apple pie?

4.  What were some of the more unusual ways of traveling as mentioned in the book?

5.  Would you want to take a trip like the young girl in the story?

## Related Books

Berger, Melvin. *The Whole World in Your Hands: Looking at Maps*. New York: Chelsea House, 1998.

Chambers, Catherine. *All About Maps*. New York: Watts, 1998.

Kenda, Margaret. *Geography Wizardry for Kids*. New York: Barrons Educational Series, 1997.

Knowlton, Jack. *Maps and Globes*. New York: Thomas Y. Crowell, 1985.

LaPierre, Yvette. *Mapping a Changing World*. New York: Lickle, 1996.

Petty, Kate. *Maps and Journeys*. New York: Barron's Educational Series, 1993.

Sweeney, Joan. *Me on the Map*. New York: Crown, 1996.

Weiss, Harvey. *Maps: Getting from Here to There*. New York: Houghton Mifflin, 1995.

## *Activities*

1. Provide students with opportunities to create personal and individual maps. Some may wish to create simple maps of their bedrooms at home. Others may want to create maps of their houses or immediate neighborhoods or communities. Some students may want to attempt to create specialized maps of their towns, such as maps of the shopping areas, of the entertainment areas (playgrounds, theaters, etc.), or of the community helpers (police, fire stations, etc.).

2. Invite students to make the apple pie from the recipe in the back of the book. Encourage students to list all the ingredients as well as the country of origin for each ingredient. Which countries were represented in the final pie? How did those countries compare with the countries listed in the book? Invite students to post the names of all the countries on a large wall map in the classroom.

3. Invite students to bring in several examples of road maps. Discuss with them the similarities and/or differences among the maps. Which map is easiest to use? Why? Which map is most difficult to use? Why? Which map might students use to get from their town to a place 500 miles away? Or 1,500 miles away?

4. Encourage students to create their own globes. Provide them with round balloons, newspapers torn into strips, some liquid starch, and water. Invite students to blow up their balloons, dip strips of newspaper into the starch, and wrap them around the balloons (two to three layers should be used). When the balloons are completely covered, allow them to dry for a day or two, then invite students to paint them with tempera paints.

5. Students can locate information about each of the countries mentioned in the book at the following Web site: **http://www.geographica.com**.

   Invite selected students to obtain necessary information about each country and share it with others in the class. They can obtain additional information on each of 85 countries (including photographs) from **http://lcweb2.loc. gov/frd/cs/cshome.html**.

6. If possible, invite a sailor or boating enthusiast into your classroom to explain the use of sea charts. Ask the sailor to bring several charts of a port, a channel, or an ocean. Encourage students to investigate the differences between those charts and land maps. Why are depths indicated on the charts?

7. Invite students to collect various apple pie recipes from family members. Students may wish to assemble these recipes into a class apple pie recipe book as part of an extended writing project.

8. Invite students to trace the history of the apple. Where did it originate? How long have people been eating them? How have apples been prepared in the past? How many countries in the world grow apples?

9. Students may want to obtain all the facts and figures about apples (and other fruits and vegetables) from **http://www.fandvforme.com.au/homepage.htm**. Invite them to assemble the collected data into an informative brochure about apples.

10. Obtain several compasses and take the class on a walking tour of the school grounds. Encourage students to plot locations of various sites and their positions and then invite the class to create a map of the school grounds.

11. Invite each of several small groups to select one of the countries in the book and then prepare a descriptive pamphlet on the economy and natural resources of that country. Invite students to focus on the reasons their assigned country was selected for inclusion in the book (why is the designated apple pie ingredient thought to be the best from that particular country?

12. Invite students (with their parents) to visit one or two travel agencies and collect brochures and other descriptive literature about foreign countries and other vacation spots. Invite students to bring this material into class and organize it into several categories (e.g., places northeast from our school, places more than 500 miles from our school, places where ships cannot operate, etc.). Students may wish to make several posters or collages about their findings.

13. Invite students each to take an imaginary journey to one of the countries mentioned in the book. Encourage each student to keep a journal or diary of his or her travels. Students may wish to include entries about sites seen, people met, places visited, food eaten, and transportation used.

14. Provide students with opportunities to create their own three-dimensional maps of the local community or geographical area. Following is a recipe for edible spreadable clay; this clay can be used to construct various land forms and then eaten when the activity is completed.

## EDIBLE SPREADABLE CLAY

Mix two parts peanut butter with one part honey.

Add three parts dry milk (a little at a time) until a stiff mixture forms.

The mixture should be thoroughly kneaded with hands.

Refrigerate overnight and use the next day.

15. Invite each student to draw and color the flag of one of the countries mentioned in the book. The flag can be posted in the classroom along with a brief illustration and description of the ingredient obtained from that country.

16. Invite students each to write to a pen pal in one of the countries listed in the book. They can obtain names and addresses from one or more of the following organizations:

> League of Friendship, Inc.
> P.O. Box 509
> Mount Vernon, OH 43050-0509
>
> Student Letter Exchange
> R.R. 4, Box 109
> Waseca, MN 56093
>
> World Pen Pals
> 190 Como Ave.
> St. Paul, MN 55208

17. One of the ideas mentioned in the back of the book suggests that readers hold an apple-tasting party (a party at which different varieties of apples are tested and tasted). Invite your students to an apple-tasting party—providing them (when practical) with apples from various regions around the United States (e.g., Washington, Pennsylvania, New York, etc.). Encourage students to rank each variety of apple on a large wall chart.

18. Invite students to visit a local travel agency and collect travel posters or brochures for a selected country mentioned in the book. What forms of transportation can be used to travel to the country and what are some of the sites and attractions that tourists might want to see?

# The Island-Below-the-Star

## James Rumford

(Boston: Houghton Mifflin, 1998)

## Summary

A magical tale with rich, dynamic illustrations, this story tells of five brothers and their journey across the vastness of the Pacific Ocean in search of the Island-Below-the-Star: Hawaii. Understated watercolors and a compelling text highlight this book about adventure, brotherly love, and the importance of people working together for a common goal. This story will be told and retold many times.

## Social Studies Disciplines

geography, history, sociology, anthropology

## NCSS Thematic Strands

culture; time, continuity, and change; people, places, and environment; individual development and identity; global connections

## Critical Thinking Questions

1. Why do you think the artist used watercolors for the illustrations?

2. What did you learn about sea travel that you didn't know before?

3. How is Manu similar to you?

4. How were early explorers able to travel across vast oceans without navigation equipment?

5. Would you want to make a voyage similar to the one the five brothers made?

6. What do you find most interesting about ocean travel?

## Related Books

Feeney, Stepanie. *A Is for Aloha*. Honolulu, HI: University of Hawaii Press, 1985.

Fradin, Dennis. *Hawaii: From Sea to Shining Sea*. New York: Children's Press, 1994.

Nunes, Susan. *To Find the Way*. Honolulu, HI: University of Hawaii Press, 1992.

Siy, Alexandria. *Hawaiian Islands*. New York: Dillon Press, 1991.

Staub, Frank. *Children of Hawaii*. Minneapolis, MN: Carolrhoda, 1998.

Wardlaw, Lee. *Punia and the King of Sharks*. New York: Dial Books for Young Readers, 1997.

## *Activities*

1. The Polynesian Voyaging Society of the University of Hawaii researches and provides information about the means by which Polynesian seafarers discovered and settled the Hawaiian Islands (and others). Your students may enjoy logging on to their informative and captivating Web site **http://leahi.kcc.hawaii.edu/org/pvs/pvs.html**.

2. Invite students to write to the Hawaii Visitors Bureau (2270 Kalakaua Ave., Suite 801, Honolulu, HI 96815) to obtain information and brochures about the state. Students may also wish to contact a local travel agency for posters, brochures, and travel information.

3. Invite students to calculate the time necessary for them to travel from their hometown to Hawaii. Encourage them to research and calculate the distance and approximate travel times for various forms of transportation. Students may want to combine several forms of transportation (e.g., car plus airplane plus boat) to arrive at their answers.

4. Encourage students to develop an imaginary time line for the five brothers' voyage. Record the time line on a very long strip of adding machine tape posted along one wall of the classroom. Students may wish to record significant events from the story and then illustrate them with watercolors.

5. Students may wish to log on to various Web sites to learn more about our fiftieth state. Here are some to get them started:

**http://www.hawaii.net/cgi-bin/hhp?**

**http://www.geobop.com/Eco/HI.htm**

**http://www.mhpcc.edu/tour/Tour.html**

**http://www.maui.net/~leodio/higuide.html**

**http://tqjunior.advanced.org/3502/**

6. If possible, invite an astronomer or planetarium director into your classroom. Invite him or her to share information with your class on how ancient peoples used the stars to calculate distances and plot their journeys across the vastness of the ocean.

7. Encourage students to write a sequel to the story. What did the brothers do after they arrived in the islands? How did they survive? Did they return to their own island to bring other people back to the Island-Below-the-Star?

8. Invite students to assemble items they would take with them if they were to set out on a long-distance voyage like the brothers. What essential foods (nonperishable) would they take? What types of clothing? What equipment or supplies? Remind students that they have limited space on their boat and may be on the water for a long time.

9. This activity will help students understand how waves are created:

*Materials*: a 9-x-13-inch cake pan, a straw, water, blue food color

*Directions*:

    a. Place the cake pan on a table and fill it about two-thirds full with water. Tint the water with several drops of food color.

    b. Hold the straw at about a 45-degree angle and blow across the surface of the water.

    c. Vary the angle of the straw several times and repeat step "b" above.

    d. Vary the force of the simulated wind through the straw.

When students blow through straws across the surface of the water, they create miniature waves. As they change the angle of the straw (and the power of the simulated wind moving across the water) they also change the size and shapes of the ripples or waves moving across the miniature ocean.

Winds blowing across the ocean's surface create ripples of waves. The size of a wave depends upon the speed of the wind as well as how far the wind has been moving across the ocean. Large waves are created when a steady wind blows great distances across the surface of the sea. Waves can also be created by undersea earthquakes and volcanic eruptions.

10. Here's an activity that will give students an opportunity to create and observe simulated waves.

   *Materials*: a clear empty two-liter soda bottle (with a screw-on top), salad oil, water, blue food coloring

   *Directions*:

   a. Fill an empty one-liter soda bottle 1/3 of the way up with salad oil.
   b. Fill the rest of the bottle (all the way to the brim) with water dyed with a few drops of blue food coloring.
   c. Put on the top securely and lay the bottle on its side. Now, slowly and gently tip the bottle back and forth.

   The oil in the bottle will roll and move just like the waves in the ocean. Students will have created a miniature ocean in a bottle.

   Waves are energy that moves through water. It is not the water that moves, but rather the energy in the water that causes waves to occur. Ocean waves are generated by the gravitational pull of the moon on the Earth's surface, the geological formation of the ocean floor, and the movement of wind across the surface of the water. Students can artificially create waves in a soda bottle and observe wave action that is quite similar to that which occurs throughout the oceans of the world.

11. Invite students to dramatize the voyage of the five brothers. They may wish to write and produce their own play or skit for other classes in the school.

12. Here's a traditional Hawaiian recipe for macadamia-coconut bread that will have your students begging for more:

## MACADAMIA-COCONUT BREAD

- ✓ 2 cups all-purpose flour
- ✓ 1½ cups shredded coconut
- ✓ ½ cup chopped macadamia nuts
- ✓ ½ cup sugar
- ✓ 2 teaspoons baking powder
- ✓ 1 teaspoon salt
- ✓ 1 teaspoon ground allspice
- ✓ 1 teaspoon ground nutmeg
- ✓ 1 teaspoon ground cloves
- ✓ 2 eggs, beaten

### (Recipe Continued)

- ✓ ½ cup coconut milk (fresh or canned), unsweetened
- ✓ ½ cup melted butter

Preheat the oven to 350 degrees. In a large mixing bowl combine the flour, coconut, nuts, sugar, baking powder, salt, allspice, nutmeg, and cloves. In a separate bowl, whisk together the eggs, coconut milk, and butter. Fold the liquid ingredients into the dry ingredients. Blend thoroughly. Pour the mixture into a lightly greased 9-x-5-inch loaf pan. Bake for 45 to 50 minutes or until a toothpick inserted in the center comes out clean. Place the bread on a rack and allow to cool slightly. Serve to a very appreciative class.

13. Invite students to share stories about journeys, trips, or vacations they have taken. What makes those trips so memorable? Why do people travel? What is the fascination of a new destination? Students may wish to assemble their memories (and responses to the questions) into a travel notebook for display in the classroom.

14. Invite a sailor (professional or recreational) to your classroom to describe some of the things he or she must do when preparing for a voyage. How is the trip planned? What precautions are taken? What supplies or equipment are taken? Students may wish to compare the visitor's preparations with those of the five brothers in the story. What are the similarities or differences?

# Lon Po Po: A Red Riding Hood Story from China

**Ed Young, translator**
(New York: Philomel, 1989)

## Summary

In the countryside of northern China, a woman lived with her three daughters. One day, because she had to leave the house to visit her daughters' granny, she warned her children not to open the door or let anyone in. Soon after her departure, a wolf visits the house in the disguise of the grandmother. With wit and wisdom, the three children are able to dispatch the wolf. This is a marvelously illustrated Chinese version of the classic tale *Little Red Riding Hood.*

## Social Studies Disciplines

sociology, anthropology

## NCSS Thematic Strands

culture; individual development and identity

## Critical Thinking Questions

1.  What are some of the similarities between this story and the story of Little Red Riding Hood? What are some of the differences?

2.  Did you know what was going to happen to the wolf before the end of the story? What clues were there in the story?

3.  Do you think the three girls were clever? What did they say or do that made you believe they were wise?

4.  The illustrations are painted in Chinese style. What did you enjoy most about them? How do they differ from illustrations in other books you have read?

## Related Books

Coerr, Eleanor. *Sadako.* New York: Paper Star, 1997.
Louie, Ai-Ling. *Yeh-Shen: A Cinderella Story from China.* New York: Paper Star, 1996.
Olaleye, Isaac. *Bitter Bananas.* Honesdale, PA: Boyds Mills Press, 1996.
Rumford, James. *The Cloudmakers.* Boston: Houghton Mifflin, 1996.
Wolkstein, Diane. *White Wave: A Chinese Tale.* New York: Harcourt Brace, 1996.

Yolen, Jane. *The Emperor and the Kite*. New York: Paper Star, 1998.

Young, Ed. *The Lost Horse: A Chinese Folktale* New York: Silver Whistle, 1998.

———. *Mouse Match: A Chinese Folktale*. New York: Harcourt Brace, 1997.

## *Activities*

1. Invite students to retell the story from the perspective of the wolf. What were some of the things the wolf observed or thought about? How would the wolf's version of the story be different from a version told by one of the three daughters? Or the version as told by the narrator?

2. Part of the story concerns ginkgo nuts. Although these are not commonly available in most grocery stores, you and your students may want to obtain several different varieties of other nuts (for example, walnuts, cashews, pecans, Brazil nuts, etc.). Invite students to taste these and then rate them according to taste. Which ones did they enjoy the most? Which ones did they enjoy the least?

3. Obtain a copy of *Yeh Shen: A Cinderella Story from China,* which is illustrated by Ed Young (see above). How does Yeh Shin compare with the version of Cinderella your students are most familiar with? Are there any comparisons between that book and *Lon Po Po*?

4. Students may wish to work together to create a large wall mural recounting important scenes from the story. Obtain a large sheet of newsprint from a local hobby store or newspaper office. Using tempera paints, students can work together to illustrate the scenes. Be sure the finished mural is displayed for everyone to enjoy.

5. Students may be interested in listening to a self-advancing slide presentation (with audio) of the original version of *Little Red Riding Hood*. They can do so by logging on to **http://www.ipl.org/youth/StoryHour/goose/ridinghood/**.

6. Students may be interested in obtaining the most current information about China. They can do so at the following Web sites:

   **http://www.chinatoday.com**

   **http://www.nationalgeographic.com/resources/ngo/**

   **maps/view/images/chinam.jpg**

   **http://www.kiku.com/electric_samuri/virtual_china/index.html**

   **http://www.globalfriends.com/html/world_tour/china/china.htm**

   **http://lcweb2.loc.gov/frd/cs/cntoc.html**

7. Invite students to create a diary (titled *Day in the Life of a Chinese Student*) based on library investigations and information obtained from the Web sites listed above. What does a Chinese boy or girl (at the same age as your students) do during the course of a typical day? How is her or his school day different from or similar to an American student's day? You and your students may wish to construct oversized Venn diagrams of the information on large sheets of newsprint.

8. Invite students to look at several examples of books that Ed Young has illustrated. What features or characteristics do students note in his work? What special qualities have made him a Caldecott Award winner? Invite students to replicate some of his illustrations in their own styles. Students may wish to make their own interpretations of *Little Red Riding Hood* for display in the classroom.

9. Encourage students to form themselves into a theater troupe and act *Lon Po Po* for other classes. Your students may wish to visit grades lower than yours and share the story with younger students. Or they may wish to put together a video production, which they can later contribute to the school library.

10. Invite your students to assume the roles of newspaper reporters and to report on the events in *Lon Po Po* as though they were part of the local newspaper. What might be some significant events, background information (real or imaginary), or photographs (illustrations) that could be included in a *Lon Po Po* newspaper?

11. Invite students to write a letter to real or imaginary pen pals about their imaginary lives in China. What do they do each day? What are some of their chores or obligations? How are their weekends spent? What do they routinely see or do? Students may wish to collect samples of these letters together into a classroom notebook.

12. There are several versions of *Little Red Riding Hood* throughout the world. Some students may enjoy producing the following humorous readers theatre version of the story for their classmates or students in another classroom.

# *Little Red Riding Hood and the Big Bad Wolf Have a Friendly Conversation (Finally)*

## *Staging*

The narrator sits far behind the two characters. The characters can stand in front of the audience or sit on two tall stools (see figure 10.1).

```
Narrator
   X

            Little Red Riding Hood        Big Bad Wolf
                      X                         X
```

**Fig. 10.1. Staging for *Little Red Riding Hood and the Big Bad Wolf Have a Friendly Conversation (Finally)*.**

**Little Red Riding Hood:** (*happily*) Hi, my name's Little Red Riding Hood and I'm the star of this story. First of all, let me explain something to you. You'll probably notice that the narrator is sitting way back there she points. We thought about it for a long time and decided that a narrator really wasn't necessary for this story. It's not that we don't like narrators—they're actually pretty nice—it's just that we felt like giving the narrator a break in this story and doing it ourselves.

So, anyway, this is the story of how I listen real carefully to my grandmother before I go to visit her on the other side of the forest. It's also about a meaningful conversation I have with the Big Bad Wolf—the same guy who used to harass little girls and break into old people's homes. But this time around he's a whole new individual! Just watch.

**Little Red Riding Hood:** (*on the telephone*) That's right, Granny. I'll be real careful when I come to visit you. I'll look both ways when I cross the street, I won't talk to any strange creatures along the way, and I'll make sure I leave my house in plenty of time to arrive at your house before dark. Oh, and yes, I'll be sure to carry a can of mace with me, too. Bye, bye, Granny. I'll see you soon.

**Narrator:** (*to audience*) You know, I was just thinking. This story just isn't going to work out like it should if there's no narrator. So, if it's all right with you guys, I think I'll just jump in here and see if I can help this story along.

(*to audience*) By now you know that Red Riding Hood is off on her visit to Granny's house. And you also probably know that she's going to meet Big Bad Wolf along the way. So let's all get back into this story and she how Red Riding Hood handles herself in the forest.

**Little Red Riding Hood:** (*singing to the tune of "It's a Beautiful Day in the Neighborhood" [also known as "Mr. Rogers's Neighborhood" theme song]*) It's a beautiful day for a forest walk, a beautiful day for a forest, we should watch out, we should watch out, we should watch out for strangers.

**Big Bad Wolf:** Hey, little girl, what are you doing?

**Little Red Riding Hood:** Obviously you're not too bright, wolfman. You must be familiar with this story by now. Can't you see that I'm on my way to Granny's house?

**Big Bad Wolf:** Oh, yeah, right! I guess I kinda forgot. You know it's been such a long time since I've been in this story.

**Little Red Riding Hood:** So anyway, fur face, what have you been up to lately?

**Little Red Riding Hood:** (*to audience*) Now look, don't be too surprised at my attitude toward this guy. He's just a wolf, not your usual story creature with long teeth and blood dripping down his face. It's not like this guy is scary or anything. He's just a wolf. A big dumb wolf. Certainly nothing to get excited about.

**Big Bad Wolf:** (*to Little Red Riding Hood*) Well, you see, I've been spending time with my brother lately trying to get him to a doctor. You probably met him in another story . . . he's the one with asthma. Yeah, whenever he gets around straw or sticks or even bricks he always feels like he's got to huff and puff. It's really cutting down on his social life and certainly making the local police quite suspicious of his actions. I'm trying to get him some allergy tests, but so far I haven't been too successful.

**Little Red Riding Hood:** Well, the next time you see your brother, please give him my best. I think that with a little medical help he might be able to control his heavy breathing and begin to assume a more normal lifestyle—like killing defenseless sheep and stuff like that.

**Big Bad Wolf:** Yeah, thanks, I'll tell him you said *Hi*. By the way, what have you got in your basket there?

**Little Red Riding Hood:** Oh, just a couple of new CDs for my Granny, a few MTV videos, and some chocolate chip cookies. You know how lonely it can get out there in the middle of the forest. So I thought I'd bring along some entertainment to help her pass the time away. Say, by the way, how would you like to do me a favor?

**Big Bad Wolf:** Name it.

**Little Red Riding Hood:** Well, as you know, Granny is awfully lonely, she doesn't get many visitors—you know what a bad reputation this forest has. Would you mind dropping in on her every once in a while? Nothing special, just a friendly visit. Of course, there can't be any funny stuff like in the last story—no putting on her pajamas or eating her up. Those things really bother her.

**Big Bad Wolf:** No problem. I'd love to drop in and chat. It gets pretty lonely in the forest for us animals, too. After all, all I usually get to do is eat a few rabbits, growl a little, and sleep for most of the day. I'd love to be able to visit Granny every so often. She's good company.

**Little Red Riding Hood:** Then it's done. I guess I'd better be on my way, now. Granny will be expecting me. And since you're not going to eat me or my Granny in this story, I don't have to worry about you any more. But, maybe I'll see you the next time I'm through these woods.

**Big Bad Wolf:** Yeah, take care. Hope to see you soon!

**Narrator:** Unbelievable. I guess the Big Bad Wolf has finally turned over a new leaf. From now on, it looks like he's going to be a productive member of society and an outstanding citizen of the forest. It may even change the outcome of other fairy tales, too. I'll call the three little pigs next week and let you know what I find out.

Reprinted from Anthony D. Fredericks, *Frantic Frogs and Other Frankly Fractured Folktales for Readers Theatre* (Englewood, CO: Teacher Ideas Press, 1993).

13. Students will notice that many of the illustrations of the wolf in this book are dark and ominous. Invite students to collect other pictures and illustrations of wolves from a variety of old magazines. Encourage them to create a wolf collage to post on a classroom bulletin board. Discuss how wolves have been portrayed throughout history. Why do people typically view or illustrate wolves as evil creatures?

14. Invite students to collect personal stories and recollections of times in their lives when they have been clever. Encourage students to reflect upon personal events and circumstances in which they had to use their cleverness or intelligence to get out of a sticky situation. You may wish to discuss the relationship between cleverness and common sense.

15. Invite students to investigate other books or literature collections containing folk tales and stories from China. Encourage students to share those stories with classmates or with students in other classes. What makes Chinese folk tales so distinctive? How are they different from traditional European folk tales?

# Appendix A

## An Annotated Bibliography of Children's Literature

The number of books available in social studies is limitless. My own investigations led me to thousands of literature possibilities—many of which could be easily integrated into all aspects of the social studies curriculum. Obviously, no book this size can do justice to the scores of literature selections you can choose for your program. I have, therefore, tried to provide you with a variety of possibilities: old favorites and classics as well as new and fascinating books for every part of your social studies program. There's something for everyone.

This appendix contains two annotated bibliographies. The first is a collection of books organized according to the seven basic concepts of all social studies curricula: self, family, community, city, state, nation, and world. The second bibliography is a selection of books arranged according to the six major topics of social studies: geography, anthropology, sociology, political science, economics, and history. Any one book may, of course, encompass more than one concept as well as more than one topic. There are also many more books in your school library or community library. In other words, the organization of books within each of the two bibliographies may be arbitrary and certainly arguable. Nevertheless, I hope these selections offer a plethora of potential literature selections for *all* areas of your social studies curriculum—no matter what its scope, sequence, or instructional emphasis.

## The Concepts of Social Studies

### Self

Adoff, Arnold. *Hard to Be Six*. New York: Lothrop, Lee & Shepard, 1991.
   A six-year-old discovers how tough life can be when his older sister has a birthday.

Anholt, Lawrence. *What I Like*. New York: Putnam, 1991.
   Six children share the different things they like to do.

Bunting, Eve. *Moonstick: The Seasons of the Sioux*. New York: HarperCollins, 1997.
   A young boy begins his journey towards manhood in this wonderfully retold legend.

Hewett, Joan. *Hector Lives in the United States Now: The Story of a Mexican-American Child*. New York: Lippincott, 1990.
   As a recent immigrant to Los Angeles, Hector experiences many things in his new country. What he learns and how he deals with life in the United Sates is beautifully told.

Levinson, Marilyn. *The Fourth-Grade Four*. New York: Henry Holt, 1991.
   Alex needs glasses, but isn't sure if the glasses will prevent him from playing soccer.

Mendez, Phil. *The Black Snowman*. New York: Scholastic, 1989.
   A black snowman and a magic cloth help a young boy appreciate his ethnicity and own self-worth.

Naylor, Phyllis. *Shiloh*. New York: Atheneum, 1991.
> The story about a boy who stands up for his principles in the face of the grown-ups' decisions.

Polacco, Patricia. *Just Plain Fancy*. New York: Bantam Books, 1990.
> Naomi, an Amish girl, finds a fancy egg and makes an amazing discovery about herself.

Ringgold, Faith. *Tar Beach*. New York: Crown, 1991.
> Cassie dreams about life in this rich and brilliantly illustrated book.

Waddell, Martin. *Once There Were Giants*. New York: Delacorte, 1989.
> Full of illustrations, this book depicts the growth of a girl from infancy through adolescence and then to adulthood.

## *Families*

Beatty, Patricia. *Bonanza Girl*. New York: Morrow, 1962.
> A delightful book about a family's journey from Oregon to Idaho in the 1880s.

Croll, Carolyn. *The Three Brothers*. New York: Putnam, 1991.
> Three brothers race to see who can fill a barn to its fullest.

Curtis, Christopher. *The Watsons Go to Birmingham*. New York: Delacorte, 1995.
> A humorous story about a summer vacation in 1963. A sure-fire winner!

Day, Nancy. *The Lion's Whiskers*. New York: Scholastic, 1995.
> In this Ethiopian story, a brave woman must pluck three whiskers from a fierce lion if she is to win the love of her reluctant stepson.

Flournoy, Valerie. *The Patchwork Quilt*. New York: Dial Press, 1985.
> A family is brought together as they involve themselves in the construction of a patchwork quilt.

Hoffman, Mary. *An Angel Just Like Me*. New York: Dial Books for Young Readers, 1997.
> A young boy desires a Christmas angel that looks just like him. A favorite uncle accomplishes the task.

Hoyt-Goldsmith, Diane. *Arctic Hunter*. New York: Holiday House, 1992.
> The story of one summer in the life of an Inupiat Indian and how he and his family survive.

Isadora, Rachel. *At the Crossroads*. New York: Greenwillow Books, 1991.
> Children in South Africa gather at a crossroads to await the return of their fathers, who have been away for 10 months.

Johnson, Angela. *Tell Me a Story, Mama*. New York: Orchard, 1989.
> A young girl and her mother share stories about the mother's childhood.

McKissack, Patricia. *Ma Dear's Aprons*. New York: Atheneum, 1997.
> A wonderful family is beautifully portrayed in this look at life in 1900.

Mitchell, Barbara. *Waterman's Child.* New York: Lothrop, Lee & Shepard, 1997.
    Life on the Chesapeake Bay can be difficult, but a strong family makes it survivable.

Nelson, Vaunda M. *Always Gramma.* New York: Putnam, 1988.
    A grandmother gets old and must be sent to a nursing home. Her granddaughter remembers all their special times together.

Pinkney, Andrea. *Seven Candles for Kwanzaa.* New York: Puffin Books, 1993.
    A descriptive and informative book about the origins of Kwanzaa and the symbolism expressed in the seven candles.

Pomerantz, Charlotte. *The Chalk Doll.* New York: Lippincott, 1989.
    When her daughter is sick, a mother shares stories of her childhood in Jamaica.

Ray, Deborah K. *My Daddy Was a Soldier: A World War II Story.* New York: Holiday House, 1990.
    While their husband and father goes to war, a wife and daughter must work to keep the family together during trying times.

Smith, Robert. *The War with Grandpa.* New York: Dell, 1995.
    A young boy learns about his grandfather and the wisdom of age in this compelling book.

Uchida, Yoshiko. *The Bracelet.* New York: Philomel, 1993.
    An informative book about a Japanese-American family and their imprisonment in a World War II internment camp.

Vizurraga, Susan. *Our Old House.* New York: Henry Holt, 1997.
    A young girl discovers the stories and history of an old house.

## *Communities*

Climo, Shirley. *City! San Francisco.* New York: Macmillan, 1990.
    This book is a wonderful introduction to a city many adults feel is the most intriguing of any in the United States.

Craft, Ruth. *The Day of the Rainbow.* New York: Viking, 1989.
    A big city, a hot summer day, sounds and smells, and lots of people all combine to make up urban life on one particular day.

Grifalconi, Ann. *The Village of Round and Square Houses.* New York: Little, Brown, 1986.
    In the village of Tos in the Cameroons, the women and children live in round houses and the men live in square houses.

Lucas, Eileen. *Peace on the Playground: Nonviolent Ways of Problem Solving.* New York: Watts, 1991.
    Examines the peaceful resolutions of problems in everyday situations.

Martin, Jacqueline. *The Green Truck Garden Giveaway.* New York: Simon & Schuster, 1997.

> A group of people become a working community in this all-inclusive story about shared work and shared experiences.

McCurdy, Michael. *Hannah's Farm: The Seasons on an Early American Homestead.* New York: Holiday House, 1988.

> Rural life and the changing of the seasons dominate this tale of a farm family in the 1800s.

Pirotta, Saviour. *Turtle Bay.* New York: Farrar, Straus & Giroux, 1997.

> An old man and two children work together for the preservation of sea turtles in Japan.

Pryor, Bonnie. *The House on Maple Street.* New York: Morrow, 1987.

> 107 Maple Street is a special place simply because of all the people who have passed by or lived there over several years.

Robinson, Aminah. *A Street Called Home.* New York: Harcourt Brace, 1997.

> A bustling and active community from 1940 is presented in all its wonderful detail.

Schotter, Roni. *Captain Snap and the Children of Vinegar Lane.* New York: Orchard, 1990.

> A group of children care for a cranky old sailor and learn the value of friendship.

Shelby, Anne. *We Keep a Store.* New York: Orchard, 1990.

> Describes how a young black girl and her family run and operate a country store.

Smucker, Anna E. *No Star Nights.* New York: Alfred A. Knopf, 1989.

> A child looks back at how life was in a small mill town.

## States and Regions

Blake, Robert. *Akiak: A Tale from the Iditarod.* New York: Philomel, 1997.

> The excitement of the Iditarod dogsled race is presented in compelling fashion in this marvelous book.

Cooney, Barbara. *Island Boy.* New York: Viking, 1988.

> Several generations of the Tibbetts family are traced in this eloquent portrayal of New England's culture and history.

Little, Lessie Jones. *Children of Long Ago.* New York: Philomel, 1988.

> A collection of poems that describe growing up in the rural South.

Precek, Katherine. *Penny in the Road.* New York: Macmillan, 1989.

> A superb book; compares Pennsylvania life in 1913 with that in 1793.

Sandin, Joan. *The Long Way Westward.* New York: HarperCollins, 1989.

> Describes the journey of Carl Erik and his family from New York City to relatives in Minnesota.

Siebert, Diane. *Heartland.* New York: Thomas Y. Crowell, 1989.
> An extended poem that paints a beautiful picture of life in the American Midwest.

Turner, Ann. *Grasshopper Summer.* New York: Macmillan, 1989.
> The trials, tribulations, misery, and discoveries made by a young boy as he travels from Kentucky to the Dakota Territory.

## *Nation*

Beatty, Patricia. *Charley Skedaddle.* New York: Morrow, 1987.
> The story of Gettysburg told through the eyes of a 12-year-old boy.

Bierhorst, John. *The Dancing Fox: Arctic Folktales.* New York: Morrow, 1997.
> A collection of rich and compelling stories recount life in the Arctic.

Booth, David. *The Dust Bowl.* Toronto: Kids Can Press, 1997.
> Delightful illustrations highlight the accounting of life in the 1930s.

Brown, Don. *Alice Ramsey's Grand Adventure.* Boston: Houghton Mifflin, 1997.
> It's 1909 and 22-year-old Alice Ramsey sets out to cross the country by car—the first woman to do so.

Gray, Nigel. *A Country Far Away.* New York: Orchard, 1989.
> A city boy from the west and a rural boy from Africa are compared and contrasted. Lots of marvelous illustrations.

Harvey, Brett. *Cassie's Journey: Going West in the 1860s.* New York: Holiday House, 1988.
> Heading for California in a covered wagon, Cassie tells of the sights and adventures she encounters during a memorable journey.

Hunt, Irene. *Across Five Aprils.* Parsippany, NJ: Silver Burdett, 1984.
> A compelling and memorable account of one family during the Civil War. A terrific read-aloud book.

Jacobs, William Jay. *Ellis Island: A New Hope in a New Land.* New York: Scribner's, 1990.
> A thorough and enlightening history of the entry point for many Americans—from its early days to its current rebirth as a historical museum.

Jeffers, Susan. *Brother Eagle, Sister Sky.* New York: Dial Books, 1991.
> Chief Seattle tells of the importance of preserving all plants and animal life.

Kroll, Steven. *By the Dawn's Early Light: The Story of the Star Spangled Banner.* New York: Scholastic, 1994.
> Lots of information and intriguing background data about the origins of our country's national anthem.

Sneve, Virginia Driving Hawk. *The Seminoles.* New York: Holiday House, 1994.
> The history of the Seminole Indians is vividly presented in this delightful book.

Turner, Ann. *Mississippi Mud: Three Prairie Journals*. New York: HarperCollins, 1997.
This book is a collection of the thoughts and ideas of three pioneer youth as they travel westward by wagon train.

Van Leeuwen, Jean. *Bound for Oregon*. New York: Dial Books For Young Readers, 1994.
An account of one family's trek across the frontier to the promised land of Oregon.

Wardlaw, Lee. *Punia and the King of Sharks: A Hawaiian Folktale*. New York: Dial Books for Young Readers, 1997.
A delightful tale of how a small boy outwits the king of the sharks to provide for his village.

Williams, Vera, and Jennifer Williams. *Stringbean's Trip to the Shining Sea*. New York: Scholastic, 1988.
Stringbean Coe and his brother take a trip from Kansas to the Pacific Ocean. The authors tell the tale through postcards and photographs.

## *World*

Baer, Edith. *This Is the Way We Go to School: A Book About Children Around the World*. New York: Scholastic, 1990.
Readers have an opportunity to see how children their own age from many different countries start their school day.

Cherry, Lynn. *Flute's Journey*. San Diego, CA: Gulliver, 1997.
A touching and moving account of the first year in a wood thrush's life as he makes a dangerous migration.

Czernecki, Stefan. *The Cricket's Cage: A Chinese Folktale*. New York: Hyperion, 1997.
A very wise cricket plays a significant role in the design of Beijing's Forbidden City.

Delacre, Lulu. *Arroz con Leche*. New York: Scholastic, 1989.
A fascinating book, in both English and Spanish, of the songs and rhythms of Mexico, Puerto Rico, and Argentina.

Dolphin, Laurie. *Our Journey from Tibet: Based on a True Story*. New York: Dutton, 1997.
A touching and moving account of children traveling to India to avoid religious persecution.

Kandoian, Ellen. *Is Anybody Up?* New York: Putnam, 1989.
The early morning experiences of one girl and several people who occupy the same time zone from Baffin Bay to Antarctica.

Lauber, Patricia. *How We Learned the Earth Is Round*. New York: HarperCollins, 1990.
This book examines all the great explorers of the world and their fabulous adventures.

London, Jonathan. *Ali, Child of the Desert*. New York: Lothrop, Lee & Shepard, 1997.
A young boy becomes separated from his family during a violent Saharan sandstorm.

Morris, Ann. *Bread, Bread, Bread.* New York: Lothrop, Lee & Shepard, 1989.
Lots of colorful photographs show how people from different parts of the world make, eat, and share bread.

Rumford, James. *The Cloudmakers.* Boston: Houghton Mifflin, 1996.
A Chinese grandfather and his grandson work to fool the Great Sultan and invent paper in the process.

Ryan, P. *Explorers and Mapmakers.* New York: Lodestar, 1990.
A vivid description of how various explorers discovered and charted the world from early history to present day.

Say, Allen. *Grandfather's Journey.* Boston: Houghton Mifflin, 1993.
A beautiful story about a man who lives in two worlds—Japan and the United States.

Temple, Frances. *Tonight by Sea.* New York: Orchard, 1995.
This inspirational novel depicts the hardships and triumphs of a tiny community in Haiti.

# The Disciplines of Social Studies

## *Geography*

Aardema, Verna. *Bringing the Rain to Kapiti Plain.* New York: Dial Press, 1981.
The story of the effects of a terrible drought on a region of Africa that lives and dies according to the amount of rainfall it receives.

Bash, Barbara. *Desert Giant: The World of the Saguaro Cactus.* Boston: Little, Brown, 1989.
A wonderful introduction to life in the desert and the panorama of flora and fauna that exists there.

———. *Tree of Life: The World of the African Baobab.* Boston: Little, Brown, 1989.
The baobab tree, which grows on the dry savannahs of Africa, is life for many creatures.

Bellamy, David. *The River.* New York: C. N. Potter, 1988.
Life on a small river and its perils highlight this wonderfully illustrated book.

Cooper, Kay. *Where in the World Are You? A Guide to Looking at the World.* New York: Walker, 1990.
Readers are provided with numerous opportunities to understand and use maps in a variety of situations.

Cowcher, Helen. *Antarctica.* New York: Farrar, Straus & Giroux, 1990.
How humans are affecting the delicate balance of life in this wonderful ecosystem.

Kudlinski, Kathleen. *Facing West: A Story of the Oregon Trail.* New York: Viking, 1996.
The journey of one family from Missouri to Oregon in 1845.

Lesser, Carolyn. *Storm on the Desert.* New York: Harcourt Brace, 1997.
> A beautifully illustrated and poetic paean to life on the desert—before and after a summer shower.

Siebert, Diana. *Mojave.* New York: Thomas Y. Crowell, 1988.
> The beauty and vastness of the Mojave Desert are wonderfully illustrated in this book about the United States' best-known desert.

Vieira, Linda. *Grand Canyon.* New York: Walker, 1997.
> A picturesque examination of one of this country's enduring wonders.

## *Anthropology*

Ancona, George. *Mayeros: A Yucatec Maya Family.* New York: Lothrop, Lee & Shepard, 1997.
> A photodocumentary of a Mayan family living on the Yucatan Peninsula of Mexico.

Arnold, Caroline. *Stories in Stone.* New York: Clarion, 1996.
> A intriguing investigation of the art of a group of Native Americans in eastern California.

Bruchac, Joseph, and Jonathan London. *Thirteen Moons on Turtle's Back.* New York: Philomel, 1992.
> A collection of poems based on Native American legends combined with impressive illustrations make this a must-have book for the classroom.

Climo, Shirley. *The Egyptian Cinderella.* New York: Thomas Y. Crowell, 1989.
> The age of the Pharaohs is dramatically brought to life in this blend of fact and fiction about a sixth-century Cinderella.

Dawson, Imogen. *Clothes and Crafts in Aztec Times.* New York: Silver Burdett, 1997.
> A wonderful introduction to the life and times of the Aztecs of southern Mexico.

Golden, Barbara. *The Girl Who Lived with the Bears.* San Diego, CA: Gulliver, 1997.
> A delightful folk tale from the Pacific Northwest about a girl, the bears she lives with, and the disastrous results.

Hamilton, Virginia. *The People Could Fly.* New York: Alfred A. Knopf, 1985.
> A wonderful collection of African-American folk tales for every classroom.

Hoyt-Goldsmith, Diane. *Totem Pole.* New York: Holiday House, 1990.
> A Tsimshian Indian boy watches his father carve a new totem pole.

Kroll, Virginia. *With Love, to Earth's Endangered Peoples.* Nevada City, CA: Dawn Publications, 1998.
> An investigative and appreciative look at endangered people from around the world.

Lester, Julius. *How Many Spots Does a Leopard Have?* New York: Scholastic, 1989.
> A collection of engaging folk tales reflecting both African and Jewish traditions.

Onyefulu, Ifeoma. *Chidi Only Likes Blue.* New York: Cobblehill, 1997.
   A wonderful book about colors, life, customs, and practices in Nigeria. A great read-aloud book.

San Souci, Robert. *The Hired Hand.* New York: Dial Books for Young Readers, 1997.
   A well-known African-American folk tale is retold in this beautifully illustrated book.

Sewell, Marcia. *People of the Breaking Day.* New York: Atheneum, 1990.
   This book examines the original inhabitants of southeastern Massachusetts and their contacts with the pilgrims.

## *Sociology*

Ada, Alma. *Gathering the Sun: An Alphabet in Spanish and English.* New York: Lothrop, Lee & Shepard, 1997.
   Bright colorful paintings highlight this delightful collection of 28 poems.

Ashabranner, Brent. *Still a Nation of Immigrants.* New York: Cobblehill, 1993.
   This book presents a sweeping overview of immigrants and immigration in this country.

Gray, Nigel. *A Country Far Away.* New York: Orchard, 1989.
   An African boy and a boy from a Western country have more similarities than differences.

Hoyt-Goldsmith, Diane. *Hoang Anh: A Vietnamese-American Boy.* New York: Holiday House, 1992.
   A wonderful book that chronicles the discoveries and education of a young Vietnamese boy.

———. *Pueblo Storyteller.* New York: Holiday House, 1991.
   A wonderful book that looks at the life and customs of a 10-year-old storyteller.

Kandoian, Ellen. *Is Anybody Up?* New York: Putnam, 1989.
   A look at some of the people who live in the same time zone and how they begin their day.

Keegan, Marcia. *Pueblo Boy: Growing up in Two Worlds.* New York: Cobblehill, 1991.
   The compelling story of a 10-year-old Pueblo Indian boy who lives in two cultures.

Lee, Kathleen. *Illegal Immigrants.* San Diego, CA: Lucent Books, 1996.
   Addresses illegal and legal immigrants coming into the United States.

Murphy, Jim. *Across America on an Emigrant Train.* New York: Clarion, 1993.
   A wonderful story and delightful account of one man's journey across America.

Onyefulu, Ifeoma. *A Is for Africa.* New York: Cobblehill, 1993.
   A delightful and engaging alphabet book that showcases the life and times of modern Africa.

Paul, Ann. *Eight Hands Round: A Patchwork Alphabet.* New York: HarperCollins, 1991.
Illustrated patchworks keyed to each letter of the alphabet highlight this delightful book.

Sanders, Scott. *A Place Called Freedom.* New York: Atheneum, 1997.
The story of a family of freed slaves as they settle in Indiana and begin a community.

Sandin, Joan. *The Long Way Westward.* New York: Harper & Row, 1989.
A Swedish family, seeking a new life, moves from Sweden to New York and then to the Midwest.

Shepard, Aaron. *The Sea King's Daughter: A Russian Legend.* New York: Atheneum, 1997.
A wonderfully told and beautifully illustrated story about love and sacrifice.

Sneve, Virginia. *The Apaches.* New York: Holiday House, 1997.
Picturesque illustrations vividly depict this creation story from the Apache people.

Young, Ed. *Lon Po Po: A Red Riding Hood Story from China.* New York: Philomel, 1989.
An inventive Chinese version of a familiar tale. This folk story is thought to be more than 1,000 years old.

———. *Voices of the Heart.* New York: Scholastic, 1997.
A book that defies description; get one for every library and every classroom.

## *Political Science*

Adler, David A. *A Picture Book of Benjamin Franklin.* New York: Holiday House, 1990.
A straightforward biography of one of the most influential people in early U.S. history.

Osborne, Mary. *George Washington: Leader of a New Nation.* New York: Dial Books for Young Readers, 1991.
This book offers a variety of perspectives and insights about our country's first president.

Rochelle, Belinda. *Witnesses to Freedom: Young People Who Fought for Civil Rights.* New York: Lodestar, 1993.
A compelling book that examines the lives of eight young people who stood up for their beliefs.

Scholes, Katherine. *Peace Begins with You.* San Francisco, CA: Sierra Club Books, 1993.
The author shares her perceptions of peace, conflict, and resolutions in an exquisitely illustrated book.

## *Economics*

Demi. *One Grain of Rice: A Mathematical Folk Tale.* New York: Scholastic, 1997.
A young girl outwits a selfish ruler in this timeless tale of good over evil.

Field, Rachel. *General Store.* New York: Greenwillow Books, 1988.
Merchandising during the early years of the twentieth century is vividly portrayed in this well-crafted poem.

Orr, Katherine. *My Grandpa and the Sea.* Minneapolis, MN: Carolrhoda, 1990.
>    A young child learns that we must replace everything that we take from nature. Delightful illustrations.

Schwartz, David M. *If You Made a Million.* New York: Lothrop, Lee & Shepard, 1989.
>    Various sums of money from one cent to $1,000,000 are explained along with checking and savings accounts and bank loans.

Sherrow, Victoria. *Huskings, Quiltings, and Barn Raisings.* New York: Walker, 1992.
>    This book examines how early settlers worked and socialized as they created a new community.

## *History*

Adler, David. *A Picture Book of Thomas Jefferson.* New York: Holiday House, 1990.
>    An interesting look into the life and times of one of America's most prominent statesmen.

Arnold, Caroline. *Stone Age Farmers Beside the Sea: Scotland's Prehistoric Village of Skara Brae.* New York: Clarion, 1997.
>    A book about some incredible people who lived in the Orkney Islands between 100 B.C. and 500 B.C.

Blos, Joan. *A Gathering of Days: A New England Girl's Journal.* New York: Scribner's, 1979.
>    The life of a 14-year-old girl is wonderfully recounted through her diary entries.

Bryan, Ashley. *Ashley Bryan's ABC of African American Poetry.* New York: Atheneum, 1997.
>    A wonderful and engaging collection of poetry from more than 70 African-American poets.

Calvert, Patricia. *Great Lives: The American Frontier.* New York: Atheneum, 1997.
>    Fascinating stories about men and women who explored and settled the great American frontier highlight this book.

Carter, Alden. *The American Revolution: War for Independence.* New York: Watts, 1992.
>    An excellent introduction to the causes and major conflicts of the Revolutionary War.

Cohn, Amy, ed. *From Sea to Shining Sea.* New York: Scholastic, 1993.
>    A collection of songs, stories, and essays about different periods of this country's history.

Ericson, Paul. *Daily Life in a Covered Wagon.* New York: Puffin Books, 1997.
>    The day-to-day living of a family moving westward. Loads of insights.

Filipovic, Zlata. *Zlata's Diary: A Child's Life in Sarajevo.* New York: Viking, 1994.
>    A 13-year-old girl tells about growing up in war-torn Sarajevo.

Gibbons, Gail. *Trains.* New York: Holiday House, 1987.
>Exciting graphics and colorful words outline the history of trains and their influence in America.

Greenfield, Howard. *Hidden Children.* New York: Ticknor & Fields, 1993.
>A powerful account of the children who were hidden from Nazi soldiers during World War II.

Langley, Andrew, and Philip DeSouza. *The Roman News.* Cambridge, MA: Candlewick Press, 1996.
>An imaginary newspaper account of the life and times of Rome from 800 B.C. to 400 A.D.

Mochizuki, Ken. *Baseball Saved Us.* New York: Lee and Low, 1993.
>A brilliant account of how Japanese-Americans imprisoned in an internment camp build a baseball field.

———. *Passage to Freedom: The Sugihara Story.* New York: Lee and Low, 1997.
>The engaging story of how one man saved thousands of Jewish refugees from the Nazis.

Murphy, Jim. *The Long Road to Gettysburg.* New York: Clarion, 1992.
>An outstanding account of the Battle of Gettysburg and its effect on two soldiers.

Polacco, Patricia. *Pink and Say.* New York: Philomel, 1994.
>A beautifully told story of two soldiers—one white, one black—and their perceptions of the Civil War.

Powell, Anton, and Philip Steele. *The Greek News.* Cambridge, MA: Candlewick Press, 1996.
>An imaginary newspaper account of the life and times of early Greece.

Sanders, Scott R. *Aurora Means Dawn.* New York: Bradbury Press, 1989.
>A family arrives in the Ohio Territory during the early 1800s, settles on the land, and deals with all the attendant hardships of frontier life.

Sattler, Helen. *The Earliest Americans.* New York: Clarion, 1993.
>This book examines a number of ideas and theories about the earliest inhabitants of North America.

Sim, Dorrith. *In My Pocket.* New York: Harcourt Brace, 1997.
>A young girl is sent to Scotland just before the start of World War II.

Turner, Ann. *Grasshopper Summer.* New York: Simon & Schuster, 1997.
>The compelling story of a young boy and his family who move from Kentucky to the Dakota Territory.

Waters, Kate. *Sarah Morton's Day: A Day in the Life of a Pilgrim Girl.* New York: Scholastic, 1989.
>Taken from the diary of a child who lived in Plimoth Plantation in 1627, this book illustrates the similarities and differences between children then and those of today.

# *Appendix B*

## *Web Resources*

The following World Wide Web sites can provide you with valuable background information, a wealth of social studies resources, scores of up-to-date lesson plans, and numerous tools for expanding any area of social studies education. They can become important adjuncts to any literature-based social studies curriculum and can be used by teachers and students alike. Use them to keep your lessons and units fresh and up-to-date.

*Note*: These Web sites were current and accurate as of the writing of this book. Please be aware that some may change, others may be eliminated, and new ones will be added to the various search engines that you use at home or at school.

## General

**http://www.ncss.org**
> This is the home page for the National Council for Social Studies (NCSS), the professional organization for all teachers of social studies.

**http://www.afredericks.com**
> This Web site is designed to provide busy classroom teachers with the latest information, the newest activities, the best resources, and the most creative projects in elementary science. It's updated frequently with hundreds of exciting ideas.

**http://lcweb.loc.gov/coll/print/guide/**
> The Library of Congress has thousands of images available for downloading. A keyword search index helps in locating images appropriate to any area of the social studies curriculum.

**http://www.si.edu**
> The Smithsonian Institution is a repository of thousands and thousands of resources for any and all elements of elementary social studies.

**http://www.askanexpert.com/askanexpert/**
> This site will provide you and your students with opportunities to ask questions of experts in various areas.

**http://server2.greatlakes.k12.mi.us/**
> An incredible collection of teachers' resources available for downloading. Included are lesson plans, computer software, HyperCard files, news resources, thematic units, guest speakers, field trips, and student-created material resources.

**http://www.teachers.net/lessons/**

Take a lesson, leave a lesson at the Teachers Net Lesson Exchange. The lessons cover all subjects and grade levels; the site includes links to the teachers who posted the lessons.

**http://www.globaled.org**

Here is a basic resource for global and environmental education with lots of valuable information.

**http://www.pacificnet.net/~mandel/**

A wonderful place to share ideas, concerns, and questions with educators from around the world. The material is updated weekly and you'll be able to obtain lesson plans in every curricular area. Also included are teaching tips for both new and experienced teachers.

# Children's Literature Sites

**http://www.acs.ucalgary.ca/~dkbrown**

This is the ultimate compendium of literature resources. It includes book awards, authors on the Web, book reviews, recommended books, book discussion groups, children's literature organizations, best sellers, and scores of teaching ideas.

**http://www.carolhurst.com/**

This site has a wonderful collection of reviews of great books for kids, ideas of ways to use them in the classroom, and collections of books and activities about particular subjects, curricular areas, themes, and professional topics.

**http://www.scils.rutgers.edu/special/kay/childlit.html**

Here you'll find lots of resources and valuable information on how to use children's literature in the classroom effectively. The focus is on multiple genres and various methods for promoting good books to all ages and all abilities.

**http://www.users.interport.net/~fairrosa/**

Here are articles, reviews, lists, links, authors, discussions, and monthly updates about the best in children's literature and how to share it with kids. This is a great site for the always-busy classroom teacher.

**http://www.ipl.org**

This is the Internet Public Library—an overwhelming assembly of collections and resources of a large public library. This site covers just about every topic in children's literature with a great array of resources.

**http://www.ccn.cs.dal.ca/~aa331/childlit.html#review**

This site is dedicated to reviewing World Wide Web resources related to children's literature and youth services. These resources are aimed towards school librarians, children's writers, illustrators, book reviewers, storytellers, parents, and teachers.

**http://i-site.on.ca/booknook.html**

This site is a repository of book reviews for kids written by other kids. The reviews are categorized by grade level: K–3; 4–6; 7–9; and 10–12. It's a great way to find out what's popular among young readers.

**http://www.armory.com/~web/notes.html**

This site provides reviews of children's literature written by teachers and others who love kid's books. It's an electronic journal of book reviews concentrating on how well books are written and how well they entertain.

# Multicultural Connections

**http://www.stolaf.edu/network/iecc/**

St. Olaf College in Minnesota offers a free service to classroom teachers who wish to set up e-mail connections between their classrooms and partner classrooms in another country.

**http://curry/edschool/Virginia.EDU/go/multicultural/sites/education.html**

The Curry School of Education at the University of Virginia has catalogued a variety of multicultural resources, including free lesson plans and diversity resources.

**http://www.mcps.K12.md.us/curriculum/socialstd/MBD/Lesson_index.html**

The Montgomery County (Maryland) public schools have an extensive listing of multicultural lesson plans using popular and current examples of children's literature.

# Social Studies Lesson Plans

**http://ofcn.org/cyber.serv/academy/ace/soc/elem.html**

Over 130 lesson plans in social studies are available from the Academy Social Studies Curriculum Exchange.

**http://www.digicity.com/lesson/l_socstd.html**

If you're looking for more than 2,600 lesson plans in a variety of subjects and across the grades—this is your site.

**http://www.col-ed.org/cur/#sst1**

A magnificent array of various lesson plans from the Columbia Education Center (Portland, Oregon) is available at this site.

**http://www.historychannel.com/historychannel/class/teach/teach.html**

The History Channel has loads of lesson plans and activities that correspond with specific television programs.

# Virtual Field Trips

**http://dreamscape.com/frankvad/world.html**

Take your students on more than 100 virtual tours of selected cities and countries around the world.

**http://dreamscape.com/frankvad/museums.html**

Take your students on over 300 virtual tours of selected museums, exhibits, and points of special interest around the world.

**http://dreamscape.com/frankvad/us-gov.html**

Take your students on a variety of virtual tours through the United States Government including the White House, the Senate, and the House of Representatives.

# Teacher Resources by Anthony D. Fredericks

The following books are available from Teacher Ideas Press (P.O. Box 6633, Englewood, CO 80155); 1-800-237-6124; **http://www.lu.com/tip**.

1. *Social Studies Through Children's Literature: An Integrated Approach.* ISBN: 0-87287-970-4. (192 pages; $24.00)

   Each of the 32 instructional units contained in this resource uses an activity-centered approach to elementary social studies and features children's picture books such as *Ox-Cart Man, In Coal Country,* and *Jambo Means Hello.* Each unit contains a book summary, social studies topic areas, curricular perspectives, critical thinking questions, and a large section of activities.

2. *The Integrated Curriculum: Books for Reluctant Readers, Grades 2–5* (2d Edition). ISBN: 0-87287-994-1. (220 pages; $22.50)

   This book presents guidelines for motivating and using literature with reluctant readers. The book contains more than 40 book units on titles carefully selected to motivate the most reluctant readers, such as *The Three Bears, The Salamander Room,* and *Sky Tree.* Each unit includes a summary, discussion questions that foster critical thinking, and cross-curricular extensions.

3. *Involving Parents Through Children's Literature: P–K.* ISBN: 1-56308-022-2. (86 pages; $15.00)

4. *Involving Parents Through Children's Literature: Grades 1–2.* ISBN: 1-56308-012-5. (95 pages; $14.50)

5. *Involving Parents Through Children's Literature: Grades 3–4.* ISBN: 1-56308-013-3. (96 pages; $15.50)

6. *Involving Parents Through Children's Literature: Grades 5–6.* ISBN: 1-56308-014-1. (107 pages; $16.00)

   This series of four books stimulates parents' participation in the learning process. Reproducible activity sheets based upon high-quality children's books are designed in a convenient format so that children can take them home. Each sheet includes a book summary, discussion questions, and engaging activities for adults and children that stimulate comprehension and promote reading enjoyment.

7. *The Librarian's Complete Guide to Involving Parents Through Children's Literature: Grades K–6.* ISBN: 1-56308-538-0. (137 pages; $24.50)

Activities for 101 children's books are presented in a reproducible format so that librarians can distribute them to students to take home and share with parents. Each sheet includes a book summary, discussion questions, and a list of learning activities in which parents can participate with their children. These projects build strong bonds of communication between parents and children.

8. *Frantic Frogs and Other Frankly Fractured Folktales for Readers Theatre.* ISBN: 1-56308-174-1. (123 pages; $19.50)

Have you heard *Don't Kiss Sleeping Beauty, She's Got Really Bad Breath* or *The Brussels Sprouts Man (The Gingerbread Man's Unbelievably Strange Cousin)*? This resource (Grades 4–8) offers 30 reproducible satirical scripts for rip-roaring dramatics. Side-splitting send-ups and wacky folk tales are guaranteed to bring snickers, chuckles, and belly laughs into the classroom.

9. *Tadpole Tales and Other Totally Terrific Titles for Readers Theatre.* ISBN: 1-56308-547-X. (115 pages; $18.50)

A follow-up volume to the best-selling *Frantic Frogs and Other Frankly Fractured Folktales for Readers Theatre*, this book provides primary-level readers (Grades 1–4) with a humorous assortment of wacky tales based on well-known *Mother Goose* rhymes. For example, *Old MacDonald Had a Farm and, Boy, Did It Stink (E-I-E-I-O)*. More than 30 scripts and dozens of classroom extensions will keep your students rolling in the aisles.

10. *Science Adventures with Children's Literature: A Thematic Approach.* ISBN: 1-56308-417-1. (190 pages; $24.50)

Focusing on the new Science Education Standards, this activity-centered resource uses a wide variety of children's literature to integrate science across the elementary curriculum. With a thematic approach, it features the best in science trade books; stimulating hands-on, minds-on activities and experiments in life, physical, earth, and space sciences; and a host of tips, ideas, and strategies that make teaching and learning science an adventure. A delightful array of creative suggestions, dynamic thematic units in all areas of science, and stimulating new science literature and activities highlight this resource.

# Index

# About the Author

## Anthony D. Fredericks

Tony is a nationally recognized children's literature expert well known for his energetic, fast-paced, and highly practical presentations for strengthening elementary education. His dynamic and stimulating seminars have captivated thousands of teachers from coast to coast and border to border—all with rave reviews! His background includes extensive experience as a classroom teacher, curriculum coordinator, staff developer, author, professional storyteller, and university specialist in children's literature, language arts, social studies, and science education.

Tony has written more than 35 teacher resource books in a variety of areas, including the hilarious *Tadpole Tales and Other Totally Terrific Treats for Readers Theatre* (Teacher Ideas Press), the highly acclaimed *From Butterflies to Thunderbolts: Discovering Science with Books Kids Love* (Fulcrum), the rip-roaring *Frantic Frogs and Other Frankly Fractured Folktales for Readers Theatre* (Teacher Ideas Press), and the best-selling *Science Adventures with Children's Literature: A Thematic Approach* (Teacher Ideas Press).

Not only is Tony an advocate for the integration of children's literature throughout the elementary curriculum, he is also the author of a dozen children's books including *Elephants for Kids* (NorthWood), *Exploring the Oceans* (Fulcrum), *Slugs* (Learner), and *Cannibal Animals* (Watts). He is currently a professor of education at York College in York, Pennsylvania, where he teaches methods courses in social studies, science, and language arts. Additionally, he maintains a Web site **http://www.afredericks.com** with hundreds of exciting resources, dynamic activities, and creative projects for the entire elementary curriculum.

## from **Teacher Ideas Press**

### SOCIAL STUDIES THROUGH CHILDREN'S LITERATURE
**An Integrated Approach**
*Anthony D. Fredericks*

If you enjoyed *More Social Studies Through Children's Literature*, come back to the book that inspired it. Completely different activities with an abundance of new titles will lead to more great curriculum connections. **Grades K–5.**
*xviii, 192p. 8½x11 paper ISBN 0-87287-970-4*

### COOKING UP U.S. HISTORY
**Recipes and Research to Share with Children,** 2d Edition
*Suzanne I. Barchers and Patricia C. Marden*

Elementary students will delight in preparing their own porridge and pudding; making candles, soap, and ink; or trying out the pioneers' recipe for sourdough biscuits. This wonderful collection of recipes, research, and readings is divided into units that complement the social studies curriculum. **Grades 1–6.**
*xv, 203p. 8½x11 paper ISBN 1-56308-682-4*

### GEOGRAPHIC LITERACY THROUGH CHILDREN'S LITERATURE
*Linda K. Rogers*

Combining practical, student-centered activities with an annotated bibliography of more than 160 children's books, this guide models ways for classroom teachers to teach geography through children's literature. **Grades K–6.**
*ix, 161p. 8½x11 paper ISBN 1-56308-439-2*

### LITERATURE CONNECTIONS TO WORLD HISTORY *and*
### LITERATURE CONNECTIONS TO AMERICAN HISTORY
**Resources to Enhance and Entice**—*Both for Grades K–6!*
*Lynda G. Adamson*

Jump start classes and research projects by exposing students to some of the great historical fiction novels, biographies, CD-ROMs, and videotapes described in these two volumes of literature connections sure to enhance any lesson. **Grades K–6.**
*World History: xii, 326p. 7x10 paper ISBN 1-56308-504-6*
*American History: x, 542p. 7x10 paper ISBN 1-56308-502-X*

### FOLKTALE THEMES AND ACTIVITIES FOR CHILDREN
### VOLUME 1: Pourquoi Tales
### VOLUME 2: Trickster and Transformation Tales
*Ann Marie Kraus*

Traditional how-and-why stories and the magical appeal of fairy tales will attract your students to a variety of related learning experiences such as cultural explorations and nature studies. **Grades 1–6.**
*Volume 1: xv, 152p. 8½x11 paper ISBN 1-56308-521-6*
*Volume 2: xviii, 225p. 8½x11 paper ISBN 1-56308-608-5*

**For a free catalog or to place an order, please contact: Teacher Ideas Press/Libraries Unlimited at 1-800-237-6124 or**
- **Fax: 303-220-8843**
- **E-mail: lu-books@lu.com**
- **Mail to: Dept. B003 • P.O. Box 6633**
  **Englewood, CO 80155-6633**